A Legal Guide to Growing Older

Planning for Disability, Dementia, & Death

RONALD ZACK, RN, JD

Copyright © 2016 Ronald Zack, RN, JD
All rights reserved.
ISBN: 1535444681
ISBN-13: 9781535444682
Library of Congress Control Number: 2016912335
CreateSpace Independent Publishing Platform
North Charleston, South Carolina

DEDICATION

To my parents

CONTENTS

Dedication		iii
Acknowledgments		vii
Introduction		ix
Disclaimer		xi
1	Transitions	1
2	What Does Law Have To Do With It?	5
3	Pick Your Team	10
4	Six Basic Estate Planning Documents	13
5	Your Last Will and Testament	20
6	The Risk of Doing It Yourself	24
7	Probate- What's Wrong With It?	28
8	Avoiding Probate Without a Trust	32
9	Capacity or Incapcity - That is the Question	36
10	Charitable Giving	39
11	Protecting Your Beneficiaries & the Money You Leave Them	43
12	Five Basic Advance Directive Documents	46
14	Speaking of Death	51
15	Murder By Document	55
16	Guardianships & Conservatorships	58
17	Property & Casualty Insurance	62
18	Do You Have An Estae Plan For Your Facebook Account (and Other Digital Assets)	67
19	Protecting Your Pet	71
20	Choosing Your Successor Trustee, Executor or Agent	74
21	The Perils of Being a Trustee, Excutor or Agent	78
22	Planning on a Shoestring	83
23	Library Fires & Ethical Wills	86
24	Estate Planning Myths, Missteps, and Mess Ups	89
25	Hospice	93
26	What's Next?	99

Reading and Resources	105
Websites	109
About the Author	110

ACKNOWLEDGMENTS

I would like to thank my parents, Sam and Dorothy Zack, who taught me the value of a strong work ethic. I also thank my clients who have taught me about life, death, and legacy.

Additionally, I greatly appreciate the quiet support of my wife, Linda - without her patience and tolerance, I could not have completed this book. And many thanks, also, to my many colleagues, estate planning and elder law attorneys, as well as hospice nurses and administrators, who serve the public with both passion and compassion.

A special thank you to David Francis, publisher of Tucson Happenings Magazine (tucsonhappenings.com) where some of these chapters had previously appeared in a different form.

INTRODUCTION

In writing this book I use many examples from Arizona law. These examples are based on Arizona law at the time the book was written. They may have changed. Any reference to the law of other states may also have changed. I have designed the book to generally address these various topics, so there should be applicable information wherever you are. This is not a book particular to one state or another. Although estate planning laws are often state specific, there are common threads and concepts that run throughout the laws of every state.

The goal of this book is to give the reader some practical information about legal issues related to planning for disability, dementia, and death, and dealing with the crises that occur when planning was either not done or not done well. Each chapter is designed to stand alone. Read the book in any order, browse through the chapters, read what interests you at the time. The subject may seem a bit morbid to some. It doesn't have to be. What is morbid is the tragedy of not planning, and the tremendous emotional and financial costs involved.

DISCLAIMER

The information in this book should not be construed as legal advice, nor the formation of an attorney-client relationship between the author and any reader. Any results described in this book are based on facts of a specific case, or presented as a broad generality, and do not represent a promise or guarantee. This book is not intended to solicit clients for any particular attorney. Readers are strongly encouraged to seek competent legal advice from an experienced attorney in their area.

1

TRANSITIONS

*"Life is pleasant.
Death is peaceful.
It's the transition that's troublesome."*

-Isaac Asimov

Everybody dies. As a registered nurse working in emergency departments and intensive care units, I witnessed numerous deaths in the early part of my career. Most of those deaths occurred during or shortly after heroic resuscitative efforts. The patient usually experienced a cardiac arrest and we performed CPR and other intrusive and invasive measures of advanced cardiac life support - medications, intubation, cardiac compressions and defibrillation (not necessarily in that order). In the ICU, patients were often on some form of life support - mechanical ventilation, intra-aortic balloon pumps, hemodialysis, and various other assistive devices and extreme medications. I remember when, in the late 1970's, we used long intra-cardiac needles to inject epinephrine directly into the heart. I remember performing the "pre-cordial thump" - a single pound with a fist on the chest during a witnessed cardiac arrest - shown so vividly in the introduction to the "Marcus Welby, M.D." television show. I also remember "the Thumper," an archaic air-pressure driver attached to the chest to continuously administer mechanical chest compressions.

Those days were full of excitement. During a "code," doctors would perform cut-downs to find veins (a surgical exploration of an area), or insert subclavian or femoral central lines through the upper chest or groin. Sometimes we used externally applied temporary pacemakers to keep an injured heart beating. The bed would be covered with empty syringes, often with needles stabbed into the mattress to keep count of the meds we gave. A technician would be up on the bed doing compressions, while nurses worked on starting IVs on both arms, and sometimes the feet. Meanwhile, a respiratory therapist would be ventilating with an Ambu bag while runners stood by to take specimens to the lab. A doctor or nurse would be probing the wrist with a needle trying to get an arterial blood sample to check arterial blood gases. One person was in charge of watching the monitors and calling out changes. Doctors shouted out orders. The nursing supervisor, holding a clipboard, would be recording it all. We were sometimes successful, depending on how we measured success. For example, success in the emergency room might have been a brain dead patient with a pulse of his own, on a ventilator, ready to transfer to the intensive care unit. That was a "save." While in the intensive care unit, success might be a patient stable enough to surgically place a gastric tube for long-term feeding so she could be transferred to a general floor, and then on to a nursing home.

I did that kind of work for 20 years and loved every minute of it. I prided myself on my skills, such as quickly starting an IV in an emergency - sometimes one, two or three lines. I intubated patients (placing a tube into the trachea), inserted urethral catheters (to drain urine), prepared drugs, recognized cardiac arrhythmias, and followed the American Heart Association ACLS protocols for each situation. I liked the drama. I was flattered and honored to be interacting with patients in their most intense and intimate moments (at the end of life) as I did everything possible to ward off the demon death. Anything was better than having the patient pronounced dead and having to tell the family it was over. In fact, I often felt that our job was to not let the patient die in the ER. To never have to tell the family it was over.

Back then, it seemed the rule was to preserve life by delaying death. There was a presumption that people wanted to live at any cost. Of course, there was the Karen Ann Quinlan case in 1976, in which the court allowed the young woman to be taken off a ventilator. A number of similar cases followed; cases like Nancy Cruzan and Terri Schiavo were some of the more highly publicized ones. All of these cases raised awareness regarding life-prolonging measures, quality of life, and the financial and emotional expenses of keeping people alive when the likelihood of recovery was small. We began to examine what people's wishes actually were, and how they could be carried out, and by whom.

The Patient Self Determination Act, establishing an individual's right to decline life-sustaining treatment, was not passed until 1990. Since then, many people have become aware of the issues surrounding prolonged life sustaining treatment at the end of life. There is still, however, considerable misunderstanding among the general population, legal professionals, and even among health professionals, about when life sustaining treatment is appropriate and when it is not.

In the 1990s, I changed my nursing focus to hospice. Hospice in the United States was relatively new at that time, and Medicare payment for hospice care had been fairly recently introduced. This seemed like an opportunity for me to impact patients and families in a very different way. In acute care, especially in the emergency department, I rarely had the opportunity to develop relationships with patients and their families. They were in and they were out. Hospice was different. I considered hospice care to be nothing short of revolutionary. Our focus in hospice was on comfort care for the dying patient and the grieving family. I was often called upon in a crisis to try to manage symptoms that had spiraled out of control. We emphasized a good death and quality of life over quantity of life. As a hospice nurse I was privileged to be present with the family at many deaths, usually in the patients' homes. Quite different from the cold and chaotic hospital settings.

Hospice utilizes an interdisciplinary approach. The team includes a doctor, nurse, home health aide, social worker, chaplain, bereavement counselor, volunteers, and often other therapists. The team works together to manage physical, social, spiritual, and emotional issues. Each team member draws upon a different set of skills, and coordinates each service with the others. Generally, the hospice nurse acts as case manager coordinating care.

One thing I learned from hospice is that all physical symptoms can be managed. No longer does anyone need to physically suffer at the end of life. We have the tools and the knowledge to make everyone comfortable, but we don't always have those tools and that knowledge available. Unfortunately, even when available, we don't always use them. Making sure tools are available and utilized is our challenge. I cannot emphasize enough, though, that physical suffering at the end of life can be effectively managed. We can also effectively manage spiritual, emotional, and psychological issues in the dying patient and her family through the interventions of the various hospice team members. The tools available include a number of sophisticated medications and methods of delivering those medications. These deal not only with pain, but with symptoms like nausea, fatigue, anxiety, agitation, disorientation, dizziness, and excess secretions. We use a variety of delivery methods ranging from oral, sublingual, rectal, subcutaneous, intravenous, inhalation, and even injections into the spinal column. In extreme circumstances, forms of anesthesia can be used. All of these tools, however, require sophisticated knowledge and significant experience to be used effectively.

In addition to dealing with physical symptoms, team members such as psychologists, social workers, counselors, therapists, and chaplains are often highly skilled at working with patients and families who are dealing with the full array of end of life issues. Many professionals are focusing their practices on these issues. Still, the field of hospice and palliative care is in its early childhood and although the knowledge base is large, the number of knowledgeable practitioners is relatively small. There is much that needs to be done.

2

WHAT DOES LAW HAVE TO DO WITH IT?

As a hospice nurse, I found we were able to manage all types of symptoms at the end of life. Physical symptoms, social, emotional and spiritual troubles could all be effectively addressed. The tools and knowledge were available, and just needed to be utilized in every case. But I always felt something was missing.

Despite the advances in hospice and palliative care, the one thing we could not seem to do anything about was any legal issue facing the patient or the family at the end of life. Often, I would encounter a terminally ill head of household whose biggest worry was that he had not planned for his family. These patients were often terrified that a spouse or dependent child would not have adequate resources or simply would not know what to do after their death. They were sometimes afraid their family would fight over their assets or that settling their affairs would be very costly. These are real fears that can often be eliminated by proper planning. People often feel a great sense of relief and comfort after completing estate planning documents. Many refer to that feeling as "peace of mind." As hospice professionals, the most we could do was give them state forms for advance directives, or a commercial pamphlet.

Many people tell me one of the most important things to them, and one of their biggest concerns regarding their death, is that their survivors not have a hard time sorting out their affairs and transferring their assets. They have seen their friends' spouses struggle, and their friends' kids fight. They have sometimes heard stories or seen friends' estate assets swallowed up in attorney fees, court costs, and probate litigation. They have seen or heard stories of families split apart by bitter fighting among heirs and potential heirs. And if they haven't seen someone they know personally go through it, they certainly have heard the many stories of celebrity deaths that have resulted in disaster for survivors.

In hospice, we do not have tools to deal with these law-related end-of-life issues. There is no attorney on the interdisciplinary team. As health professionals, we have often developed a healthy, and often justified, fear of lawyers. Lawyers represent medical malpractice lawsuits, and are often considered the enemy. We are reluctant to involve an attorney, share information with an attorney, or even expose our patient to an attorney. As a hospice nurse, this presented a problem to me. This problem was a major reason I decided to become a lawyer and focus my practice on helping people prepare for legal issues related to the end of life (disability, dementia, and death), and on helping patients and their families when they had not prepared.

Why is it important that people prepare for legal issues related to the end of life? I have already mentioned the need for survivors to navigate the myriad of tasks required after death, including wrapping up the affairs of the decedent and distributing assets. People frequently tell me they want their wishes followed in regard to their care if they become incapacitated, they want their wishes followed regarding the disposition of their remains, and they want their assets distributed in a certain way. They want their estate to pay the least possible in taxes, expenses, and legal fees. These goals can be accomplished through planning. Proper planning can greatly reduce cost after death.

I often tell people that 70% of my practice is estate planning and 30% is litigation. In other words, 70% of my clients come to me to plan. In that realm, I am meeting with clients and drafting wills, trusts, powers of attorney, and other estate planning documents. I am often reviewing clients' current or older documents, researching legal issues concerning individual estate planning needs, and evaluating clients for potential of exploitation, undue influence, and capacity. Often, I visit clients in their home, hospital, nursing home, or inpatient hospice unit.

The other 30% of my clients involve cases in litigation. This consists of preparing for and going to court for guardianships, conservatorships, will contests, trust disputes, estate administration issues, and the like. More often than not, these cases deal with fighting among family members: adult children who don't get along, stepchildren vs. stepparent, brother vs. brother, and any other imaginable combination. Interestingly, about 70% of my income comes from that 30% of my client base. Litigation is extremely expensive for clients and extremely lucrative for attorneys. Going to court, preparing for court, and completing all the tasks required by the rules and statutes is very costly. I have seen small estates with 30 or 40% of the estate value swallowed up by legal fees. Proper planning can often avoid the need to involve courts, and often can eliminate the future need to involve lawyers.

Sometimes people tell me they don't need planning because they "don't have much." Many people think estate planning is for the wealthy. Nothing could be farther from the truth. Planning is extremely important for smaller estates because of the need to preserve as much money as possible. For example, planning for funeral expenses of a few thousand dollars may preserve several thousand dollars that could otherwise be exhausted in fees and expenses of administration. Even with very little assets, it is important to remember that estate planning consists of so much more than how assets are distributed after death. There is a wide array of planning needs surrounding asset management during a period of disability, or decision making regarding health care, placement, and treatment. All of these are aspects of an effective estate plan.

In addition, you don't know when you will die, how you will die, or what you will have when you do die. One case I dealt with involved an elderly gentleman who had a very small estate just before he died. He was struck by a car and killed. The driver's insurance paid the limits of their policy to his estate. He also had an accidental death life insurance policy tied to a credit card. It was one of those very inexpensive policies that pay a lot of money in the event death results from some type of accident. The proceeds of that policy also paid to his estate. He ended up with a sizeable estate going through probate.

People also tell me they are too young for estate planning. Many think estate planning is for old people. Again, this is not true. Everyone 18 years old and over needs an estate plan of some sort. Remember, Karen Ann Quinlan was 21years old and Nancy Cruzan was 25 years old when they each entered the national spotlight.

Many children stay home until they finish college or longer. Parents can now keep children on their health insurance plan until age 25. But the parents do not have legal authority to obtain health information or to make legal or healthcare decisions if the child is unable to after the age of 18. For parents to retain that authority, the child must name the parents in a power of attorney I was involved with a case of a young man in his early 20's who suffered a head injury in a motorcycle accident. He still lived at home with his parents and attended a local college while working full time. The parents had to go to court to be appointed guardian and conservator to be able to make the necessary medical and financial decisions for their child who was now a young adult. Without a written document, the only route is through the courts, in what can be a long and expensive legal ordeal. Had the adult child completed documents appointing his parents as power of attorney for health care and finances, the court action would probably not have been necessary. Thousands of dollars could have been saved. I encourage everyone turning 18 to have these documents prepared as part of their estate plan.

A question I am often asked is whether estate planning needs to be done by an attorney. I used to tell people it is better to have some plan, any plan, even a do-it-yourself plan, rather than no plan. If you could not afford an attorney, I used to say, you were better off to try one of the do-it-yourself options and take your chances. After being on one side or the other in so many lawsuits involving estate plans, I no longer say that. I now believe in many cases, it is actually better to have no plan. If there is no plan, the statutes are very clear in what needs to be done and the law will be followed. There is little to dispute. However, if a will, for example, is poorly written, there may be many areas to litigate. If you prepare your documents yourself because you cannot afford to hire an experienced estate planning attorney to prepare the plan, I suggest buying an hour of an attorney's time to review and comment on what you have prepared. That hour can go a long way to assure your wishes are carried out the way you want.

I also encounter many people who have documents obtained from financial advisors, accountants, or non-lawyer trust and estate services. These documents are legal documents. There are many reasons things can go wrong, cost money, and cause great heartache. If you obtain estate planning documents from a non-lawyer, it is again wise to have them reviewed by an attorney, an experienced estate planning attorney.

One exception to the need to hire an attorney is health care directives. Most states provide forms compliant with that state's laws. For health care directives, and particularly a health care power of attorney (health care proxy), I suggest the state form will be fine. There is no reason for everyone not to have a health care power of attorney or healthcare proxy form completed. This is the form naming someone to make medical decisions for you if you cannot make those decisions yourself. There are other commercially available forms, some distributed by healthcare providers. I do not recommend those commercial forms. I only recommend the state-designed or sanctioned form. It is also fine to use the hospital's form when you are admitted to the facility, but that form may only be applicable for that facility. The state advance directive forms of almost every state can be obtained online at caringinfo.org, a website of the National Hospice and Palliative Care Organization

3

PICK YOUR TEAM

Estate planning is a team effort. There are actually two teams – the team that creates the plan and the team that implements the plan. Usually, there is considerable overlap between the two. Let's begin with a description of the team that will create your plan.

The team creating the plan will consist of you, and typically an attorney, and maybe your financial advisor and banker. When a plan is created, it is important to consider the titling of assets and the beneficiary designations of assets. In most cases, it is at the time of creation that you will be changing the title of assets, the beneficiaries of assets, or both. With a trust-based plan you will likely be transferring title of investment accounts, savings accounts and checking accounts into the name of the revocable living trust (RLT). It should NOT be necessary to close the account and open a new account in the name of the RLT. If the banker or account manager requires you to close the account and open a new one, I usually recommend closing the account and opening a new one at a different bank or investment company. You want advisors and bankers who are reasonable and cooperative because this will assure smooth transitions at all stages.

Choosing an attorney is sometimes difficult. You want an attorney who either specializes or focuses their practice on the area of estates and trusts. Most states have a specialization in this area. California, for example, has certified specialists in Estate Planning, Trust, and Probate Law. In Arizona, an attorney can become an Estate and Trust Certified Specialist. To obtain these designations, the attorney must demonstrate significant experience and knowledge in the area, obtain references, and pass an examination. These specialists are also required to maintain the certification with mandatory continuing legal education in this field.

On a national level, the National Association of Estate Planners and Councils (NAEPC) offers a professional designation as an Estate Law Specialist. This designation requires a certain level of experience, continuing legal education, recommendations of colleagues, and an examination.

If the attorney has been designated a specialist by the state or NAEPC, or if the attorney has been admitted as a Fellow of the American College of Trust and Estate Counsel, it is a good indication they are serious practitioners in this area. The American College of Trust and Estate Counsel is an elite group of seasoned professionals and being accepted as a Fellow is a significant accomplishment for any Estate Planning Attorney. If none of these apply, however, there are other indicators to consider in selecting your estate planning attorney. Even without these designations, you can find good estate planning attorneys.

There are, for example, a few membership organizations that can indicate the attorney is focused and probably current and active in the area of estates and trusts. These are organizations such as WealthCounsel®, the National Network of Estate Planning Attorneys, and the American Academy of Estate Planning Attorneys. Membership in any one of these organizations suggests the attorney has made a significant investment in his or her education, has the resources to keep current, and devotes a fair amount of time to this type of work.

Of course, you will also want to look for other activities that indicate the attorney's commitment. Is the attorney active in the community? Does the attorney provide education to the community or to other attorneys? Does she actively participate in local professional groups regarding estate planning? Ask friends for references. Ask other attorneys. Remember estate planning is not just about the documents but about the guidance and advice your attorney will give you.

Once this research is done, meet with the attorney. Even the best qualified attorney may not be a good fit for you. Your attorney must be someone who you are comfortable with, who you communicate easily with, and who will be available for you. Sometimes you can attend a talk the attorney is giving. Sometimes you will want a consultation. Some attorneys charge for the consultation appointment and some don't. If they do, it is usually money well spent. You will either learn it is the person for you, or not. Both are valuable lessons.

The implementation team consists of you, your attorney, your financial planner, possibly your banker, an accountant, or tax advisor, and all of the "helpers" named in your documents, such as the personal representative (executor), successor trustee (if you have a trust), your health care agent, and your financial power of attorney. These are the people who will make sure the plan is put into operation at the time it is needed, usually when and if you become incapacitated or when you die. While you are alive and well, you will remain in charge and coordinate any team members necessary, often with assistance of your attorney.

The financial advisor and banker are necessary to make sure assets such as bank accounts and investment accounts are titled properly. The financial advisor and banker can also help to confirm the appropriate beneficiary designations, pay on death, and transfer on death designations are done. It is usually a good idea to make sure your successor trustee, personal representative (executor), agents, and powers of attorney know their roles. Some attorneys have workbooks and workshops for "helper" training or "successor trustee" training. The helper should know where to go for guidance "at the time." It is, however, never too soon to prepare for these roles and learn the responsibilities that go with them.

For both teams, choosing the estate planning attorney is the most important step you can take and should be the first. The attorney will set everything into motion to meet your goals and requests and see to it that everything is completed properly. The attorney's expertise in these matters should save you and your family potential distress from poorly written or executed estate planning documents. It is worth the time and the money to make a thoughtful choice from the get go.

4

SIX BASIC ESTATE PLANNING DOCUMENTS

The belief that estate planning is only for people with a lot of money is a common misconception. Nothing could be further from the truth. Everyone should do some form of estate planning. If not, the State has done an estate plan for you, and, like many things the State does for you (or to you), you might not like it. An estate plan that you have created serves the purpose of seeing that your wishes and desires are followed concerning your money, your property, your health care and your family. Additionally, a properly designed estate plan can provide for the transfer of non-financial assets, such as your values, wisdom, and knowledge (see the chapter Library Fires and Ethical Wills for examples).

Some people are unclear what an estate plan is. The basic idea behind an estate plan is:

A plan that (1) allows a person to be in control of their assets and decision-making while they are alive and well, (2) provides instructions for caring and treatment for himself and his loved ones if he becomes disabled (incapacitated), (3) after his death gives what he wants, to whom he wants, when he wants, and in the way he wants, (4) pays the least in taxes and fees, (5) and allows the efficient and effective transfer of financial and non-financial wealth.

An estate plan can be fairly uncomplicated, expressing your desire of how you would like to be treated in the event of a serious illness and who you want to care for your minor child, or even your pet.

Six basic documents can serve as the foundation for your estate plan. Although most of these can be prepared without an attorney, it is always wise to seek the advice of a competent and experienced estate planning lawyer who can help you be sure your wishes will be carried out with the least expense and headache for your survivors.

Remember, your estate plan only deals with two things: everything you own and everyone you care about. Depending on your situation, this may be worth paying a reasonable fee. If you cannot afford to pay an attorney, there are often options available for pro bono help. Or consider buying an hour of an estate planning attorney's time to review the plan you prepared.

1. Last Will and Testament

A will is a written document in which you identify what you'd like done with your assets upon your death. The will can also name a guardian for your minor children, and sometimes for incapacitated adults. In fact, for young couples, the guardianship feature of a will is often the most important part. Even if you don't have minor children, if you have an incapacitated unmarried child or an incapacitated spouse, you can appoint a guardian in a will in Arizona and many other states.

A will can be a fairly uncomplicated document, but can also include complex trust language to provide financially for minor children or pets, and can even provide sophisticated tax planning and multi-generational transfers for larger estates. A trust created in a will is called a testamentary trust. Wills may include additional instructions, requiring the Personal Representative (Executor) to seek and obtain additional benefits, such as VA burial benefits.

A problem with a will is that it often must go through probate, although that will depend on the amount of assets and some other factors involving how assets are titled. Probate can be costly and time consuming, but that is not always the case. Unless carefully drafted, a will may be subject to dispute or wishes may not be followed due to idiosyncrasies of state law and/or vague or inconsistent drafting.

An experienced estate planning attorney can sometimes help avoid probate even with a will-based estate plan (see chapter Avoiding Probate Without a Trust).

2. Living Trust

A revocable living trust is a contract that holds title to and allows a designated trustee to control your property. The trust is a very useful document that can provide detailed instructions for how your affairs should be handled in the event of your disability, incapacity or death.

Many people have used trusts to decrease estate tax liability and to avoid probate. While it is true that trusts are very useful for estate tax planning, most people no longer need that type of planning because of changes in the federal law. In 2016, for example, the first $5,450,000 of assets are exempt from federal estate tax. Of course, many states have lower thresholds for estate or inheritance tax (there is no such tax in Arizona), and the federal law is always subject to change. Also, the issue of avoiding probate is not as significant as it once was. While some some states seem to have higher costs and more complex probate practices, most states are not that bad that probate avoidance alone is a good reason to have a trust.

The fact that a trust can provide instructions for the management of your affairs if you are incapacitated is, in my opinion, a strong advantage of a trust over a will. Unlike trusts, wills are only effective after death. A trust allows someone to easily step in and manage your affairs if you cannot.

Also, within a trust it is possible to easily create sub-trusts for the distribution of property, offering many protections over assets transferred to beneficiaries. These are particularly useful if planning for someone with special needs, someone very young or someone with other issues such as alcoholism or substance abuse. Of course, it is also possible to create testamentary trusts for devisees and legatees (beneficiaries) of a will. These can be just as useful, after your death, as sub-trusts created within a revocable living trust. Often, however, if a will is going to include effective testamentary trusts for various purposes, the cost of the will may approximate that of a trust. One of the disadvantages of a trust is that it is usually costlier to prepare than a will.

Another problem with living trusts is that it is important to make sure all your assets are placed in the name of the trust for the trust to be effective during lifetime, and possibly after death. Otherwise, the trust instructions have no bearing on those assets titled in some other way. Many people spend a lot of money to design detailed trusts that ultimately prove useless because very little gets titled in the name of the trust. Whenever you have a living trust, you also must have a pourover will. During your lifetime, you attempt to include most of your property in your trust, either through titling the property in the trust's name, assigning the property to the trust, or making the trust the beneficiary of the property. The trust includes your instructions for how the trust property will be distributed after your death. If, however, anything is missed and not in the trust at the time you die, a pourover will is necessary to transfer that property into the trust so it can be distributed according to your instructions in the trust. The pourover will simply leaves the property to the trust to be distributed according to the trust instructions.

Remember, though, a pourover will (as with any last will and testament) is not effective in transferring property if the property has another mechanism to transfer it. For example, jointly owned property will pass to the joint owner, and property with a pay-on-death designation to an individual will be distributed to that individual. Only property that would otherwise go to your "estate" will be poured back into the trust, in which case a probate will likely be required to effect that transfer. And any property that passes through the will, if it meets the legal threshold (in Arizona, more than $75,000 in personal property or $100,000 in real estate) will require a probate – even if it is pouring into a trust! The trust is considered the beneficiary of the will. After the assets are transferred to the trust, they will be distributed according to the instructions in the trust.

3. Financial Power of Attorney

A financial or general power of attorney allows a person you designate (your agent or attorney-in-fact) to access and control your financial assets.

Those powers can take effect immediately, or they can "spring" into effect if an event you define triggers its implementation. That triggering event is most often incapacity or unavailability.

A problem with a financial power of attorney is it provides the authority for someone to control your assets as if they were you, but provides few, if any, instructions for how you want them to manage those assets. The powers are often so broad the financial power of attorney has been called a "license to steal." Although Arizona, and virtually all states, has severe penalties for the misuse of these powers. Many offenders operate under the radar and never get caught. Often the abusers are family members and the abused are too embarrassed or protective to report the abuse.

Another problem with financial powers of attorney is financial institutions cannot be forced to accept them. Instead, the agent under a power of attorney, or some other person, may be forced to go to court and be appointed as conservator. A well drafted general power of attorney will nominate the agent as a court- appointed conservator, should the need arise.

The term "durable" in a power of attorney means the POA is effective even if the principal (the person who wrote it) is incapacitated. Unless the document indicates it is "durable," the law assumes it is not effective if the principal is incapacitated. Additionally, the POA is always ineffective after death.

4. Health Care Power of Attorney

The Health Care Power of Attorney identifies the person you would like to make medical decisions on your behalf. Usually, this document becomes effective if and when you become unable to make or communicate such decisions yourself. This person (agent) will be able to make any decisions regarding your person, including placement decisions.

It is very important you communicate to the person designated how you would want to be treated in the event of various medical situations. The agent under your Health Care Power of Attorney is required to make the decisions you would have made had you been able. Many people never discuss with the proposed agent the types of health care decisions and placement choices they desire. If your agent does not know what you would have wanted in a particular situation, they are required to do what they believe to be in your best interest.

It is possible for a Health Care Power of Attorney document to fail. This can happen if the healthcare provider has reasons to doubt the validity of the document. This may occur when there is a dispute in the family and a family member accuses another of influencing the patient to sign against their will, or is using a revoked document.

If the healthcare provider refuses to follow the direction of the appointed agent, or if there is some problem or question with the document, it could become necessary for a guardian to be appointed by the court. A well-drafted Health Care Power of Attorney will indicate who that guardian should be and that nomination will often be respected by courts. Some states use a separate form for nomination of guardian if that becomes necessary in the future.

Like any POA document, a Health Care POA is usually ineffective after death. Some states, however, like Arizona, have statutes that allow a principal to grant the agent certain powers that survive death. Such powers often concern disposition of remains, autopsy, and organ donation.

5. Living will

Typically, in your living will, you tell people what you want done if you need life-sustaining medical treatment to keep you alive. This document usually indicates what, if any, extraordinary measures - such as artificial hydration or nutrition, mechanical ventilation, or cardiopulmonary resuscitation - you would want if you are in a terminal condition, irreversible coma, or vegetative state, and/or the doctor believes that life-sustaining treatment will only prolong the moment of your death. Sometimes, two physicians are required to agree that life sustaining treatment is futile, depending on the document's language. In some Living Wills other types of instructions are given. For example, Jehovah's Witnesses will usually include a directive for blood transfusions to be refused under any circumstances.

The Living Will and Health Care Power of Attorney are often referred to collectively, as Advance Directives.

6. HIPAA Authorization

A Health Insurance Portability and Accountability Act (HIPAA), authorization allows medical professionals involved with your care to discuss your medical condition and provide medical record information to individuals you designate. This includes your Health Care Power of Attorney and often your Financial Power of Attorney. Without this release, medical personnel may refuse to provide the agent with the necessary information to make an informed decision about your healthcare. The HIPAA authorization can be either a separate document or a clause in the Power of Attorney.

The Health Care Power of Attorney and living will can be registered through the Arizona Secretary of State so health professionals can access them online through a password-protected account. Many states have similar registries. In Arizona, other documents, such as a Mental Health Care Power of Attorney and a Pre-Hospital Medical Directive (DNR) are also available and are discussed in the chapter Five Basic Advance Directive Documents. That chapter also includes additional information about the Health Care Power of Attorney, Living Will, and HIPAA Authorization. For other states, check the website caringinfo.org for information about each state's advance directives.

Remember that estate planning is not really about documents. It's about results. If the documents don't accomplish your goals, they are useless. Also, the documents are not useful if no one knows about them. It is a good idea for anyone named in the healthcare documents, at least the first agent, to have a copy, as well as your health care providers. Take copies if you are going into the hospital or having an outpatient procedure. As always, seek the advice of an experienced estate-planning attorney who will listen to you, learn about your situation, and be willing to teach you how to apply the law to your particular situation to achieve your desired results.

5

YOUR LAST WILL AND TESTAMENT

Statistics show the majority of the population has not made a will. Just because you haven't mad a will doesn't mean you don't have one. If you have not written a will, or done some other form of estate planning, your property will pass by intestate succession. In other words, if you don't have a will, the State has one for you. The problem is the State may not do things the way you would have done them yourself. Also, any property not provided for in your will or through other planning will follow the State's intestate succession laws; so even if you have a will, the state may still decide where some of your property goes. One of the most important reasons to have a will is to name guardians of minor children or incapacitated adult children, or an incapacitated spouse.

All states have fairly similar schemes of how your property will be distributed if there is no will. Here is what Arizona, a community property state, has planned for the disposition of your property (citations refer to Arizona Revised Statutes and are provided as examples):

If you are married, all of your separate property and your half of the community property will pass to your spouse, as long as you have no children (or no descendants - grandchildren, great grandchildren, etc.). If all of your children are also the children of the surviving spouse (the kids you've had together) then all of your separate property and your share of community property still passes to your spouse. The idea is the kids will eventually get it. (A.R.S. 14-2102(1)) If you or your spouse had children from another relationship, and if those children were adopted by the stepparent, they will be treated as the children of that relationship.

If you have children who are not also the children of your spouse (and have not been adopted by your spouse), your spouse will get half of your separate property and none of your half of community property. (A.R.S. 14-2102(2)). The rest goes to your children from another relationship.

If there is no surviving spouse (or any property that does not pass to the surviving spouse under number 2, above), property flows, in this order, to:

a. Your descendants – children, children's children, etc., through the generations.
b. If no descendants, your parents.
c. If no descendant or parent, to the descendants of your parents (your siblings, nieces and nephews, etc.)
d. If no descendant, parent or descendant of a parent, then grandparents or descendants of grandparents (your uncles, aunts and their kids, etc.). (A.R.S. 14-2103)
4. Then to the State. (A.R.S. 14-2105). The term for property going to the state is "escheat."

It is very rare that property would pass to the State – usually, there is somebody among parents or grandparents and their descendants – all your siblings, nieces, nephews, cousins, etc. Still, your property may pass to people you hardly know, don't know, or even worse, people you were not particularly fond of. The law also defines how shares are to be distributed and requires that relatives of half blood (step-relatives) inherit the same as if they were whole blood relatives. (A.R.S. 14-2107).

Some people say they are not concerned with distribution because they do not have much money, property or other material assets. Keep in mind this situation can change, even after death. The younger you are, the more likely the death will be accidental. If so, there may be someone else liable, in an automobile accident for example, and such liability could result in a large payment to your estate. There are cases of medical malpractice or product liability that cause serious illness or death and result in large awards to estates of deceased people. In that event, either your will or the State's will control the distribution.

Another problem with not having a will involves minor children. In a will, a parent can appoint a guardian of an unmarried minor. If both parents are dead, or one is dead and the other incapacitated, the appointment will become effective upon filing the named guardian's acceptance with the court. A minor over the age of 14 can object to the appointment of the guardian. (A.R.S. 14-5202 and 14-5203).

Without a will naming a guardian, Child Protective Services (Department of Child Safety in Arizona) could assume jurisdiction over the placement of a minor child, and relatives and friends could become involved in a contested guardianship proceeding in court. It is important to note that the naming of a guardian in a will is only effective if both parents are dead or one is dead and the other incapacitated. This raises issues for single parents and divorced parents of minor children. It is not unusual the custodial parent feels the surviving parent is not an appropriate person to gain full custody. In such a situation, it is important to seek legal counsel to try to avoid that result.

Wills can vary in their complexity. It is possible to build trusts into wills (testamentary trusts), to do tax planning, and to provide for distributions to be made over time, or to provide some degree of asset protection for beneficiaries. A will, however, can be fraught with perils. For example, courts will follow the statutes very carefully as to how a will must be drafted and executed (signed). If formalities are not followed, the court will not consider a will valid. Formalities include things such as how the will is signed and witnessed – based on state-specific laws. Issues such as the capacity of the person making the will or undue influence by others may arise.

A will is necessary if you want to disinherit certain relatives. Arizona law, like the laws of most if not all states, contains some exceptions, exemptions and allowances that cannot be avoided by writing a will. Usually there are minimum amounts that must be given to a spouse and minor children. These allowances reflect reflect the public policy of requiring some provisions for spouses and dependent children.

Writing a will is not a do-it-yourself project. Your estate plan deals with everything you own and everyone you care about. It makes sense to do it right to make sure you get the result you desire. An attorney, experienced in estate planning and knowledgeable of your state's statutes, should be consulted to ensure what you want can and will happen after your death. At the very least, have an experienced estate planning attorney review any document you prepare on your own.

6

THE RISK OF DOING IT YOURSELF

Do-it-yourself estate planning has gained in popularity with the proliferation of online forms and store-bought will and trust kits. Specifically, such products appear to be easy and cost-effective ways to complete a will or a trust. They are not, however, without significant risk. In 2014, the Florida Supreme Court published an opinion, Aldrich v. Basile, that points out a few of the hazards of do-it-yourself estate planning and issues a stern warning from the Justices. In this case, not only was the intent of the decedent thwarted, but the legal fees were many times the cost of a properly designed estate plan prepared by a knowledgeable and experienced attorney.

The case involves a woman, Ann Aldrich, who wrote a will on an "E-Z Legal Form." She followed the directions and wrote out instructions that her listed possessions would go to Mary Jane Eaton (her sister), or if Mary Jane Eaton died before Ann, to James Aldrich (her brother). Ann listed her house, the contents of the house, her IRA, life insurance, an automobile and her bank accounts. The list included everything Ann owned. The will was properly witnessed and signed. Ms. Mary Jane Eaton died before Ann and left Ann real estate and approximately $122,000 dollars. After Mary Jane's death, Ann wrote a document titled "Just a Note" and kept it with her will. In the note, she stated it was an addendum to her will and that all her worldly possessions would pass to Mr. Aldrich. She signed it, but did not have it witnessed. Therefore, it was not a valid codicil (amendment to a will). To be valid, a codicil must follow the same formalities as a will regarding signature and witnesses.

Ann did not have a spouse or children. After her death, Ann's nieces from a deceased brother came forth. They were not mentioned in her will. The nieces claimed they were entitled to the property that Ann received after she had made the original will. Because Florida has a statute stating that a will should be construed to pass all property owned by the testator at the time of death, including property acquired after the will was drafted, Mr. Aldrich argued he was entitled to all the property because he was the only remaining devisee/legatee (person named to receive property in a will. The case was presented and the trial court agreed with Mr. Aldrich, deciding all the property would go to Mr. Aldrich. The nieces appealed the decision and the First District Court of Appeal sided with the nieces. Mr. Aldrich then appealed and the case went to the Florida Supreme Court.

The Supreme Court agreed with the First District. It is true a will can transfer property that was not owned by the testator at the time the will was drafted and executed. To do so, however, requires a general bequest, such as a residuary clause. Such a clause would indicate the testator's intent to transfer after-acquired property. Without a residuary clause, property that was acquired after the will was made will pass by laws of intestacy to the heirs at law. So, any property not effectively distributed by the will must be distributed according to the laws of intestate succession. Intestate succession is simply the law which states who gets your property if you die without a will. It is the will the State has prepared for you and takes effect if you have not prepared a valid will or if no will can be found. This is a case where a portion is transferred by the written will and another portion transferred by the law of intestacy.

A court, in determining the intent of the testator, will only consider the "four corners of the document." Only if there is ambiguity in the language of the will, will the Court consider other evidence, outside of the will, such as testimony. Ann's will was not ambiguous and the Court found she clearly did not intend for property not specified to be distributed through the will.

What about the amendment she wrote? Because it did not meet the required formalities (witness signatures, etc.) it could not be considered at all. The court will only consider the stated intentions in a valid document. So, without a residuary clause stating that the residue, any property left after all other distributions are made, go to Mr. Aldrich, the residue passes according to the laws of intestacy and not through the will. The language of the amendment would likely have been effective had it been included in the will or properly executed as a codicil.

There is an interesting concurring opinion by the Chief Justice. She wrote that although the opinion was correct under the law, it did not seem to adhere to the testator's true intent. There is a distinction between "true" intent and "stated" intent. The court, as mentioned earlier, can follow only the stated intent. The chief justice, in her concurring opinion, wrote:

"While I appreciate that there are many individuals in this state who might have difficulty affording a lawyer, this case does remind me of the old adage 'penny-wise and pound foolish.' Obviously, the cost of drafting a will through the use of a pre-printed form is likely substantially lower than the cost of hiring a knowledgeable lawyer. However, as illustrated by this case, the ultimate cost of utilizing such a form to draft one's will has the potential to far surpass the cost of hiring a lawyer at the outset. . . . I therefore take this opportunity to highlight a cautionary tale of the potential dangers of utilizing pre-printed forms and drafting a will without legal assistance. As this case illustrates, that decision can ultimately result in the frustration of the testator's intent, in addition to the payment of extensive attorney's fees —the precise results the testator sought to avoid in the first place."

I agree with the chief justice. I used to tell people it is better to have a store-bought or on-line will, than no will at all, because something is better than nothing. I no longer believe that. Because a poorly drafted or incomplete estate plan can be very costly, both financially and emotionally,

I now feel it is better to have no plan then it is to have a substandard plan. Substandard plans can lead to tens of thousands of dollars in litigation, damaged relationships and serious emotional trauma. If there is no plan, you can simply follow the straightforward plan the State provides.

One of my colleagues recently wrote he loves do-it-yourself will kits because they represent job security for future estate litigators. While many of these plans will work just fine, you don't know which ones won't. And when they don't work, the cost of litigation can quickly escalate.

Overall, it makes great sense to spend a few extra bucks for an attorney, get it done right, and save your loved ones the money and the misery of asking the court system to clear up ambiguities and settle disputes. Even if you do not want to pay an attorney to draft the entire plan, hire one to review the one you have.

7

PROBATE- WHAT'S WRONG WITH IT?

Probate is treated as a dirty word. Many, if not most of my clients, tell me that one of their primary estate planning goals is to avoid probate. They then ask, "What is probate, anyway?" Probate is something most people know they don't want, even if they don't know what it is.

So what is it? In this context, we are speaking of what I call "death probate," or the type of legal action that may follow a death. It is a process by which a court will provide some degree of supervision and oversight to the administration of a decedent's estate. The level of supervision can vary widely. In most cases in Arizona, probate is informal and involves filing papers in court and, hopefully, never attending a hearing. Hearings are scheduled to make sure deadlines are met, but they are considered "non-appearance" hearings where no one shows up. The court uses that time to make sure the proper papers have been filed, proper notice given, and no objections have been made. Alternatively, probate can require a high level of court supervision, with every action requiring court approval. The spectrum includes everything in between.

The reason for probate is to protect creditors, heirs, beneficiaries, devisees, legatees, and anyone else who may have an interest in the estate. This is not always a bad thing.

Probate is designed for wills. Wills are designed to be "probated." Traditionally, the primary way to avoid probate is to use a Living Trust. There are, however, many ways to avoid probate even without a trust (see the Chapter Avoiding Probate Without a Trust). If there is no will (and no trust) then the probate process is also used to appoint a Personal Representative (Executor) and oversee the administration of the estate, if necessary.

I used to tell people they wanted to avoid probate for three reasons: it costs too much, takes too long, and it's very public. I will address each point. I use examples from Arizona law, but most states are similar.

1. Costs Too Much

Probate usually involves a few hundred dollars in filing fees. For example, in Pima County, Arizona, at the time of this book publication, the filing fee is $193. Other fees may include certification of papers and a bond for the Personal Representative (PR). In most cases, the bond requirement can be waived by the language of the will or agreement of parties involved. The PR may charge a reasonable fee for their time, and the attorney may charge a reasonable fee. What is reasonable can vary widely. I have seen PR's charging anywhere from $15/hour to $50/hour or more.

In my experience, attorney hourly rates in Arizona often range from $150/hour to over $300/hr. Some attorneys charge a flat rate, particularly for uncontested estates. Over the past few years, I have seen rates starting at approximately $2,500 for uncontested probate actions. A few attorneys in Arizona charge a percentage of the value of the estate. Sometimes, the language of the will specifies the payment amount or method of payment for the PR.

It is possible for people to represent themselves in Probate Court. Many jurisdictions offer state and even county-specific forms on a court website or through a legal bar association. Sometimes there is a law school or court library that offers forms, or other types of court-related self-service options.

Some states, like California and Nevada, have statutory maximums that attorneys and PR's can charge based on a percentage of the total estate. It is safe to say the cost of a probate in Arizona will likely be a few thousand dollars or more depending on whether there are objections, creditor problems, difficulty locating people, and a variety of other factors. Overall, though, the cost is often not much higher than that of a properly administering a trust. With a trust there is very little, if any, supervision or oversight unless someone takes it into court. It is possible that administering a trust will cost as much as administering a will if it is done properly.

2. Takes Too Long

The length of time to settle an estate through probate in Arizona is not as long as many think. An uncomplicated probate can be ready to close well within a year. The court expects a probate to be closed within two years, or an explanation is required. Many payments and distributions can be made before the time of closing.

In the Arizona probate procedure, known creditors must be notified directly and a notice to inform unknown creditors must be published in the newspaper once a week for three consecutive weeks. The prescribed waiting period for creditors to present their claims is four months after the date of the first publication. After four months have passed there is little concern about unknown creditors coming forward, if they do, in most cases it is too late for them. The probate can be closed after the four month creditor period.

If the probate is closed informally, there is another one-year waiting period for the PR to make sure nothing else comes up. If administering a trust, however, and there has been no publication for creditors (it can be done in some states, but is not required), the statute of limitations may be two years or longer and creditors can show up very late.

3. Too Public

One of the advantages of a trust is it can often be kept very private. Unless the trust finds its way into court, the general public cannot see the distribution pattern or any of its details. A will is different. The will becomes a matter of public record. Arizona courts, however, like many others, have implemented a number of privacy features keeping some financial records such as inventories and accountings, and sensitive information such as social security numbers, out of sight. The probate process is not nearly as public as it used to be.

So, probate does not necessarily cost too much, take too long, or violate privacy. In fact, in some cases, probate is a better choice, even if not required. Sometimes probate becomes necessary in order to reach certain assets or resolve disputes. Without court supervision, abuses may occur. Each case is unique. It is always worthwhile to get the opinion of an attorney experienced in this area to decide whether avoiding probate is the best strategy for your situation.

8

AVOIDING PROBATE WITHOUT A TRUST

In Arizona, probate is generally required if the decedent's estate has more than $75,000 in personal property or $100,000 in real property. Most states have similar thresholds. The personal property amount includes tangible personal property such as artwork, collectibles, furniture, and automobiles, as well as intangible property such as cash, any investments, and all types of accounts. Real property includes homes, land, buildings, and mines. Only equity is counted in the threshold amount, so if there is real property, the amount of any mortgages are subtracted from the value. Value is often determined by what is indicated on the current year's property tax assessment rolls. If the total amounts fall below the statutory thresholds, the property can often be transferred by a small estate affidavit without going through the probate procedure of appointing a Personal Representative and following the court process (A.R.S. 14-3971). In Arizona, these procedures require a 30 day waiting period from the time of death for personal property transfers, and six months waiting time for real property.

Even when probate is not required because the amounts are below the threshold, you can still file for probate if there is some benefit. For example, even if there is real property with equity less than $100,000, it might be more practical to file an informal probate in order to sell the property without having to wait the six months required by statute to transfer the property without a probate.

But what if there is property over the threshold amount and you want to avoid probate? We know one way to avoid probate is with a revocable living trust. But probate avoidance alone is not a reason to have a trust.

The value of a decedent's estate, subject to probate, only includes property that does not pass to the heirs through another mechanism. The key to avoiding probate is to get as much property as possible to transfer "outside of probate." There are many methods to accomplish such transfers, which are often referred to as a transfer of property "by operation of law." In other words, the property transfers automatically, without court action. This, however, requires planning.

One way property transfers by operation of law is through joint ownership. If accounts are held jointly, they will usually pass to the surviving owner(s) upon the death of the other joint owner. This often is the case with bank accounts and investment accounts. Financial institutions usually require nothing more than a death certificate to change the title of the account to the surviving joint owner(s).

In the case of real property, jointly owned property will transfer to the survivor(s) as long as the property is owned jointly with right of survivorship. In Arizona, that may be referred to as either "joint tenancy with right of survivorship" or "community property with right of survivorship." The community property option, of course, is only available to married couples. In cases with right of survivorship, the survivor or survivors must record a death certificate and an affidavit terminating the joint tenancy with the County Recorder. Real property can also be owned jointly as "tenants in common." If the deed does not indicate a right of survivorship, it is likely held as tenants in common. In that case, the survivor owns half the property and the decedent's estate will own the other half. The decedent's share does not transfer automatically, and may require probate without other planning.

Another way to transfer property to avoid probate is through beneficiary designations. This is, in fact, the most common way to transfer retirement accounts and life insurance. It is extremely important to periodically confirm your beneficiary designation is properly recorded with the financial institution. If you do not have a beneficiary designation on file, the funds may then be left to your estate, in which case they will likely have to go through probate. To avoid this, the beneficiaries should be living people, a trust, or a charity and there should always be a secondary or contingent beneficiary in the event the first one fails. Keep a copy of beneficiary designation forms with your documents.

Other types of accounts can also have beneficiary designations. Usually bank accounts will have the option of a Pay On Death (P.O.D.) designation, while beneficiary designations on investment or brokerage accounts are often referred to as Transfer On Death (T.O.D.). Either of these requires a death certificate to be presented to the financial institution for the beneficiary to obtain the funds. In Arizona, we can also transfer real estate by beneficiary designation. A "Beneficiary Deed" is used for this purpose (A.R.S. 33-405). At the time of publication, approximately 26 other states also have such a deed. It is simply a deed indicating the owner conveys the property to a specified person, people, trust, charity, or other entity upon the death of the last remaining owner. A beneficiary deed has no effect during the lifetime of the owner. In Arizona, the transfer of the property to the beneficiary occurs upon recording the death certificate.

Because so many people own property in several states, it is good to note that not every state has a provision for beneficiary deeds. Some call the deed something else, like a "transfer on death instrument (TODI)" and a few states accomplish a similar goal by using a somewhat more complicated technique called an "enhanced life estate deed" or Lady Bird Deed. If an out of state property does not permit any of these methods, a joint tenancy with right of survivorship, lifetime gift, or a revocable living trust should be considered. Otherwise, you can end up with a probate in one or both states.

Motor vehicles, on the other hand, can be easily transferred in Arizona by an affidavit (Non-Probate Affidavit) provided by Arizona Motor Vehicle Division (MVD) if certain criteria are met. Better yet, you can utilize the MVD Beneficiary Designation form. This is a form designed to transfer the vehicle upon the death of the owner, much like the Beneficiary Deed transfers real property. The form is available online and must be filled out, signed, notarized and kept with the title. Automobiles, however, count toward the $75,000 personal property threshold if there is no beneficiary designation. Again, this is a very state-specific issue and it is important to check the law of your state.

While transferring property by beneficiary designation or title is often a quick and easy way to transfer property, it is not without its dangers. The property, when transferred to individuals, will be transferred outright and that is not always desirable. If, for example, property is transferred outright to someone with a disability who needs state or federal benefits, they may lose those benefits by receiving the property.

Also, if the property is transferred to a minor or incapacitated person, the transfer could trigger a court action for a conservatorship (or guardianship in some states) – what I call Living Probate.

There are, however, alternatives to outright distribution. Property can be left to others in a trust that can offer beneficiaries protection from creditors and predators, and also spendthrift protection, divorce protection and remarriage protection (see the chapter Protecting your Beneficiaries and the Money You Leave Them). The key to all of this is advanced planning. An attorney experienced in this area of law can help determine the best way to make transfers upon your death to those you care most about.

A word of caution about joint ownership. When a property is owned jointly, it can be at risk to creditors of either owner. This is one reason why it is usually not a good idea to add a child as a joint owner on accounts or property. If the property is to be left to that child or individual and no other, it is probably better to make them a beneficiary, T.O.D., or P.O.D.. If you just want the convenience of someone to be able to write checks or access the account on your behalf, you can use a power of attorney. Most financial institutions have a form they use for this purpose.

Remember, the beneficiary designation, T.O.D., P.O.D., or joint ownership will take precedence over a distribution in a will. For example, if you name one child as a joint owner or P.O.D. on an account, and then your will says that account is to be divided equally among your three children, the property will be transferred to the individual associated with the account and not to the ones designated in your will.

9

CAPACITY OR INCAPCITY - THAT IS THE QUESTION

Capacity and incapacity, in the legal sense, are often misunderstood terms. Generally, in a legal context, we talk about the capacity to enter into contracts and agreements, and to make other types of decisions. There is a legal standard of incapacity allowing a court to determine whether a person is incapacitated, and in need of a guardian. In Arizona, determination requires a finding that the person "...is impaired by reason of mental illness, mental deficiency, mental disorder, physical illness or disability, chronic use of drugs, chronic intoxication or other cause, except minority, to the extent that he lacks sufficient understanding or capacity to make or communicate responsible decisions concerning his person" (A.R.S. 14-5101). In other words, the incapacitated person is "incompetent" because he is unable to make responsible decisions concerning his person. Legal competency is another very specific term that may apply in cases of civil commitment to a mental hospital or in criminal cases. Those types of competence is not covered here.

In terms of incapacity for a guardianship proceeding, the court must have clear and convincing evidence that the person's decision making is so impaired that he or she cannot care for his or her personal safety, or provide necessities such as food, clothing, shelter, and medical care.

In other cases, when a guardianship is not being sought, incapacity must be determined in order to implement a successor trustee or a financial power of attorney. Usually, the document will define incapacity as being determined by a physician, two physicians or a panel of people. A typical definition of incapacity will state the individual "is unable to effectively manage his or her property or financial affairs, whether as a result of age; illness; use of prescription medications, drugs, or other substances; or any other cause."

There are also other levels of legal capacity. For example, the capacity required to enter into a contract or to make an irrevocable lifetime gift is higher than the capacity required for making a will (testamentary capacity). A person, who was determined to be incapacitated by a court, may still have the capacity to make a will. A person who is mentally ill may still be able to make a will, as long as the decisions expressed in the will are not influenced by that mental illness.

There are three elements of testamentary capacity. A person who has made a will is presumed to have had all three capacity elements at the time. If someone wants to challenge capacity, they must prove one of the three elements was absent at the time the will was made. The three elements are:

1. The person must have the ability to know the nature and extent of his property. In other words, you need to know what you own.
2. The person must have the ability to know the natural objects of his bounty. In other words, you must know who would normally be regarded as the next of kin in the line of succession of your property.
3. The person must have the ability to understand the nature of the testamentary act. In other words, you need to have an understanding that the act of making a will is saying where and how your property will be distributed upon your death.

Challenging capacity after the fact is very difficult. Even if a person has dementia or a mental condition, they may very well have periods of lucidity (lucid intervals) at which time they have or had testamentary capacity. Estate planning attorneys evaluate the client's mental status to determine how to best help them write their will. Sometimes, such an evaluation requires flexibility. For example, I will sometimes schedule appointments early in the day for people who exhibit signs of dementia in the late afternoon. I also try to schedule at a time when they are less likely to be affected by medication. When I meet with a client for a will or trust, I will meet with that person alone (to avoid undue influence and make sure they are acting independently), and I write notes in the client file regarding how I determined the person had capacity. I am prepared and willing to be a witness in a will contest to testify that I evaluated the client for capacity and took measures to avoid undue influence.

I make sure the will has an attestation clause with witnesses who also attest to the person's capacity. If I have questions regarding the client's capacity, I may request a report form a physician or psychologist. Some attorneys videotape signings of estate plans as further evidence.

For all of the above reasons, it is very important that the will be prepared by an attorney with experience in this area of law. Online documents and store-bought forms are much easier to challenge. Generally, the court will give great weight to the testimony of an attorney because attorneys are considered to be officers of the court.

While challenging capacity is difficult, it is done often enough. So in preparing your will, consider the elements above. Do you have capacity? And how will it be proved, if challenged? Who will support your devisees and legatees (people you have named to receive property) when their gift is challenged?

Although we are often taught in law school that testamentary capacity is the lowest level of capacity, some courts have held that there is an even lower level of capacity required for marriage. Go figure.

10

CHARITABLE GIVING

Many people are very diligent about donating to charity throughout their lifetimes. Many of those same people, however, don't include charities in their estate plan. Usually, this is not because they don't want to, but it just had not occurred to them when they were drafting a will or choosing beneficiaries. When planning for the final disposition of an estate, most people focus on providing for spouses, children and other relatives. I think a lot more people would leave charitable bequests (gifts) if they knew how simple it is to do.

Leaving a Bequest in a Will or Trust

Naming a charity as a beneficiary in a will or trust is not only simple, but can make sure your intentions are not thwarted when a devisee/legatee (person left something in a will) or beneficiary dies before you. These gifts can be left as a specific bequest, as part of the residuary estate, or as a potential bequest for a remote contingent beneficiary.

A specific bequest, is usually a dollar amount of money, an item of personal property such as a vehicle, or a bank account. Such a gift can be simply stated in the will or trust section dealing with specific bequests:

> "My Personal Representative shall distribute [dollar amount or a phrase describing property] to [name and location of charity], or its successor in interest, for the benefit of the charity and its general purposes."

The descriptive phrase regarding the property can be a vehicle (year, make, model and VIN), property address and legal description, account name and number, shares of stock, etc. Remember to be very specific so both the charity and the property can be properly identified. Many charities have similar sounding names or multiple chapters. It is a good idea to include an address, or at least a city and state. Instead of leaving property for general charitable purposes, language can also be inserted if the money is to be used for a specific purpose or program.

There can also be a provision included to provide for the possibility of the charity either changing its name or dissolving completely. Such language may say:

> "If [name of charity] is not in existence at the time of my death and there is no identifiable successor in interest, then my Personal Representative shall designate one or more charitable organizations having the same or similar charitable purposes as [name of charity] to receive this share."

Or if you prefer, you can list another charity as a contingent or secondary choice.

A gift to a charity can also be given as a percentage or portion of the residuary of the estate, or the entire residuary amount. This applies to what is left after paying all expenses and making all specific distributions.

Lastly, a charitable gift makes an excellent "Remote Contingent Beneficiary." This only applies if some or all of the beneficiaries or legatees named in the trust or will had died before you and there was no other designated person or entity named to receive the gift. Rather than allowing your assets to go to remote relatives or even the state, it could go to a charity. Sample language: "If, at any time, there is no person or entity qualified to receive final distribution of my estate or any part of it, then the portion of my estate with respect to which the failure of qualified recipients has occurred shall be distributed to [name and location of charity]."

In my opinion, the Remote Contingent Beneficiary option should be included in every will or trust and one or more charities be considered. There is simply no downside. You avoid inadvertently leaving something to distant relatives you may not know or like, and you also avoid leaving anything to the state.

Leaving a Bequest by Beneficiary Designation

Another way to leave money to a charity is by including the charity as a beneficiary on an account, IRA, insurance policy or annuity. The charitable organization can be specified as a sole or fractional beneficiary. Usually, retirement accounts (IRA's, 401K's, etc.), life insurance policies and annuities have forms to list beneficiaries and percentages each beneficiary will receive. Banks, credit unions and investment companies also have forms to list to whom the account money will be paid on death (P.O.D.) or transferred on death (T.O.D.). In all of these cases, it is easy to list a charity as a primary beneficiary receiving a percentage, or as a contingent beneficiary. The contingent or secondary beneficiary will only receive a share if the primary beneficiary cannot or will not accept the money.

Sometimes a beneficiary will not want to receive the inheritance for one reason or another. In those cases, the primary beneficiary can disclaim the inheritance and it will then pass to contingent beneficiaries. Otherwise, if a beneficiary disclaims and there is no alternative, that money may go to someone else or even the government.

Other Charitable Giving Strategies

There are many other ways that money can be left to charities. Many of these require the assistance of an attorney or the Planned Giving department of a charitable organization. These include a variety of trusts and annuities, some of which provide lifetime income and leave the remaining amount to the charity. Such techniques can become very sophisticated and have a higher level of complexity.

It is always a good idea to speak with an experienced estate planning attorney and a financial professional to advise you on the risks and benefits of any type of charitable giving plan.

11

PROTECTING YOUR BENEFICIARIES & THE MONEY YOU LEAVE THEM

Inheritance can be left in many different ways, but there are three major methods: outright, staged distribution trust, and lifetime protective trust. One of the most common methods is to leave a sum of money "outright" or as it is sometimes it is written, "outright and free of trust." Money can be left this way in a specific bequest (e.g. "I leave my grandson, Ronald Zack, $100,000 outright and free of trust."), or it could be left as a percentage or share of an estate (e.g. "I leave the residuary to my descendants in equal shares"). After working with people inheriting money over many years, I can tell you that "outright" is usually not the best way to leave money to anyone, unless it is a relatively small amount.

A second way to leave an inheritance is in trust, to be distributed in stages. This could be a certain percentage at age milestones such as 25, 35, and 60. These instructions can be written into a trust or a will, instructing the trustee or personal representative to distribute one-third of the share at age of 25, half of the remaining amount at 35, and the balance at 60. Each stage is distributed outright, in a lump sum. The theory is the recipient matures over time and is better able to handle and protect money at older ages. This also prevents losing the entire amount at once. Other milestones can be used for a staged distribution. Graduating college, getting married, or other such events may be used as triggers for receiving a partial inheritance. Sometimes these are referred to as incentive trusts to provide an incentive to finish school or achieve some other goal.

I have read about studies demonstrating that large sums of money received outright in a lump sum often have a very short life expectancy. In fact, an often quoted study from an insurance company found a lump sum distribution would be gone in 18 months, on average, no matter what the amount. We have all heard horror stories about lottery winners going broke, and many of us have witnessed the same thing with a lump sum lawsuit settlement, or with an inheritance. For many, it is just "easy come, easy go." There are so many bright and shiny things to buy, many cool trips to take, and all those luxuries you just would love to have. And, there is a human tendency to treat money that is not earned by our own toil as less valuable.

This is not to say that everybody will go out and "blow the dough," although it happens sometimes. More often, the money is lost to some type of predator who shows up to help with investments, a business opportunity, or some other deal to double or triple the balance. Sometimes it is an outright scam. Also, friends and relatives are available with a variety of dire needs, and now that you have all this money (that you didn't really earn), you are in a better position to help.

The bigger threats, however, often come from creditors, divorce, remarriage, and lawsuits. By leaving an inheritance in what some call a lifetime protective trust, you can give your beneficiaries the gift of powerful asset protection that would otherwise be very expensive, and maybe even impossible, for them to achieve on their own after receiving the money.

We should always be concerned about large lawsuit creditors. If your beneficiary has inherited money outright, that money is always at risk of a lawsuit judgment. If, for example, that beneficiary is responsible for a car accident that caused considerable damage to property and people, like running into a school bus full of kindergarteners, it is likely the dollar amount of the damage will exceed the limits of their liability insurance. If the beneficiary has inherited assets, those will likely be taken to pay toward a judgment. If, however, the inheritance was in a lifetime protective trust created by the deceased person for the beneficiary, those assets may be protected. Other sources of creditor claims are professional malpractice lawsuits and catastrophic medical bills.

Divorce and remarriage present additional threats to an inheritance. Although, in a community property state, inheritance assets, by definition, remain the separate property of a married beneficiary, most married people quickly (or eventually) co-mingle these funds with community property. This may occur by depositing funds in a joint account, putting the spouses name on the account where the inheritance is held, or using the money to purchase assets which become community assets. The inheritance of one spouse may be considered gifts to the community depending on how it is used. The legal term is transmutation. It even sounds bad.

If you create a Revocable Living Trust, and put your assets into that trust, those assets will not be protected from creditors. If, however, you leave those assets to a beneficiary, not outright, but in the form of a trust, those assets can be given considerable protection. It is important to structure the protective trust properly. In many cases, the beneficiary can be his or her own trustee, manage the assets in trust, and make distributions to himself based on some defined standard. For instance, the IRS has identified ascertainable standards (health, education, maintenance, and support) that are often used as the standards for distribution. If the trustee, even if she is also the beneficiary, can only distribute for these reasons, there may be a high degree of creditor protection. Arrangements can be made for distributions for other reasons, often by naming an independent trustee with power to make discretionary distributions.

Inheritance money left in a well-structured protective trust is afforded very effective protections if the trust is properly drafted. It is important to consult an attorney who is familiar with these strategies and uses them with some frequency. Remember, too, that asset protection is not absolute. But leaving an inheritance in a lifetime protective trust is one of the greatest gifts you can give someone.

12

FIVE BASIC ADVANCE DIRECTIVE DOCUMENTS

Advance Directive is a term usually referring to health care directives – the planning relating to health care. Although health care is the focus, these documents also address issues like placement and personal care choices. Ideally, these documents, or at least the main document – the Health Care Power of Attorney – should avoid having to ask the court to appoint a guardian in the event of your incapacity.

In my opinion, all the other documents that are part of the Advance Directives are secondary to the Health Care Power of Attorney. All can be useful, but it is a well-written, properly executed Health Care Power of Attorney document that is the centerpiece of Advance Directives.

In order for the Health Care Power of Attorney to be effective, however, it is important you appoint an agent to make decisions for you when you are no longer able, and the appointed agent knows your wishes. Those wishes must be conveyed to the people you choose as agents, and regularly updated. Other methods apart from legal documents can be utilized to express and convey those wishes. Having a conversation about what you want, or even better, writing down what you want is necessary because most people don't normally think of all the types and categories of decisions your agent may face. Everyone, therefore, should put some effort into exploring potential options for their future health care choices. There are forms, worksheets, and workbooks designed for this purpose. I do not recommend trying to put all this information into the legal document naming your health care agent.

In addition to people knowing your wishes, it is equally important the document appointing your agent is available and accessible when needed. Remember, you might be unable to convey information in an emergency. I suggest clients provide copies of key health care documents (Health Care Power of Attorney, Living Will, and HIPAA Authorization) to each medical provider and also to each person named in the document. I also strongly recommend carrying a wallet card listing the appointed health care agent's contact information and the location of the documents.

Some people register their documents with the state (Arizona has a registry through the Secretary of State) or with a private company. Once registered, the registry will issue a wallet card with information to access documents online.

There are five main documents comprising the Advance Directives. Along with the corresponding citation to Arizona law, they are (citations refer to the Arizona Revised Statutes and are provided as examples):

1. Health Care Power of Attorney (HCPOA or MPOA); (ARS 36-3221, et seq.)
The Health Care Power of Attorney document, sometimes called a Medical Power of Attorney, identifies the individual or individuals you'd like to make medical decisions on your behalf if you become unable to make them yourself. The granted authority usually becomes effective when you become incapacitated and unable to make or communicate decisions. It can also be drafted, however, to take effect earlier.

As mentioned previously, it is very important that you communicate to the person designated, how you would want to be treated in the event of various medical events. The agent under your Health Care Power of Attorney is required to make the medical decisions you would have made had you been able, but many people never have this discussion with their proposed agent to discuss the types of health care decisions they desire.

It is always a good idea to have a separate document outlining what your wishes are. This is often done in the form of a Letter to my Healthcare Representative or a similarly titled document. The Health Care Power of Attorney may also include expanded mental health powers, either with the same or a differently appointed agent. (See also Mental Health Care Power of Attorney below.) Sometimes the Heath Care Agent is called the Health Care Proxy.

2. Living Will (LW); ARS 36-3261, et seq.)
Through a Living Will, you usually tell others what you want done if you need life-sustaining medical treatment. Most often, this document indicates if you would want extraordinary life-sustaining measures - such as artificially administered hydration or nutrition, mechanical ventilation, or cardiopulmonary resuscitation - if you are in a terminal condition, irreversible coma, or vegetative state and your death is imminent. The Living Will can be much broader, offering instructions in a wider variety of situations. If it includes too much, however, it risks causing confusion. Most often, the Living Will is the "pull the plug" (or not) document.

The Living Will can be a separate document or incorporated into the Health Care Power of Attorney. Also, the documents can indicate if the agent under the Health Care Power of Attorney or the instructions in the Living Will will prevail if there is disagreement. For example, some people like to say "pull the plug" in the Living Will, but then give their agent the authority to override that instruction if they see fit, based on what was separately expressed to them.

3. Health Insurance Portability and Accountability Act Authorization (HIPPA) (45 CFR Chapter 164)
A Health Insurance Portability and Accountability Act (HIPAA) Authorization is designed to comply with the federal privacy laws that prohibit healthcare providers from sharing information. As a free-standing document, the HIPAA Authorization can list individuals who may communicate with physicians and other providers, obtain records, or

just inquire as to your status. It does not give the named individuals any decision-making power.

A HIPAA Authorization should be built into any Power of Attorney, applying to the agent(s) named in that Power of Attorney. But because there may be others you would like listed to obtain information, a freestanding form is helpful. Also, the named agent may need access to information before the POA is effective, so all agents should be listed on the HIPAA Authorization. Sometimes, we also list any trustee and the attorney. Information for attorneys can be limited to medical information specifically related to issues of estate planning and administration, such as capacity.

Many of us have heard horror stories about a dear friend or relative who was not given any information that you were even present in a facility because they are not listed on any papers. Most often, a health care provider will ask if the person is the power of attorney. If she is not the power of attorney, but is listed on the HIPPA Authorization, she can point out to the health care provider that she is authorized to receive information about you.

4. Pre-Hospital Medical Care Directive (DNR or Orange Form)(ARS 36-3251)
The Pre-Hospital Medical Care Directive, or Orange Form, is a very specific document that applies only to first responders (EMT's, paramedics, police, fire) and emergency room personnel. The form authorizes withholding CPR- chest compressions, artificial ventilation, intubation, defibrillation and certain life support drugs. It does NOT authorize withholding IV fluids, oxygen or other treatments.

The form must be (1) printed on orange paper, (2) signed or marked by the patient or agent, (3) include a photo or identifying characteristics, and (4) signed by a licensed health care provider. This form is not appropriate for everyone. Most often, it is used by terminally ill individuals, and particularly those admitted to a hospice, although it is NOT a requirement for hospice.

It is suggested to keep the form on the refrigerator at home because responders are trained to look there. Wallet cards are also available.

The form described here is Arizona specific. Some states use a somewhat similar form that is often called P.O.L.S.T. – Physician Order regarding Life-Sustaining Treatment. This is an actual medical order that may indicate life-sustaining measures are not to be initiated in any setting.

5. Mental Health Care Power of Attorney (MHCPOA); (ARS 36-3281, et seq.)

Under Arizona law, the Mental Health Care Power of Attorney (MHCPOA) allows the appointed agent to make mental health care decisions, INCLUDING admission to a level one behavioral health facility – a locked psychiatric hospital). An agent under a regular Health Care Power of Attorney can make most other decisions related to mental health care, medications, and treatment, but not authorization for admission to a level one behavioral health facility.

The Mental Health Care Power of Attorney can sometimes prevent having to take someone to court to be involuntarily admitted to a mental health facility for court-ordered treatment. Many times, however, we have encountered difficulty getting someone to a facility against their will, even with a MHCPOA. The authorities will usually not intervene for an agent under a Mental Health Care Power of Attorney and a Petition for Involuntary Evaluation or Treatment becomes necessary. Still, I usually recommend adding this power if the person has a history of mental illness and has been court ordered into treatment in the past. Many attorneys recommend including mental health powers with every Health Care Power of Attorney.

Mental health powers can be included in a separate document or as part of the Health Care Power of Attorney. Either way, it can be written so the agent is different for the mental health powers, if you choose.

14

SPEAKING OF DEATH

Health Care providers are often required to ask about health care directives under the Patient Self Determination Act of 1990. When you are admitted to any Health Care Facility (hospital or nursing home) accepting federal money (practically any facility), you will be asked whether you have completed health care directives such as a Living Will or Health Care Power of Attorney. If you don't have any such document, the facility representative may offer forms you can use or some other type of assistance. If you do have these documents, the facility will request a copy. However, there is no requirement that you have these documents, and most people do not. A study found that only 37.2% of patients entering a hospital said they had written advance directives, and only 14.4% of those made it into the patients' records.

Having the documents, though, is rarely enough. The Living Will, if you have one, usually recites some statements about the type of care you would receive if you were unable to express yourself and certain conditions existed. For example, most Living Wills in Arizona express whether you would want life sustaining treatment like mechanical ventilation or CPR if your death was determined to be imminent. Very often, terms such as "terminal condition," "imminent death," and "incurable or irreversible condition" are vague and undefined. The Living Will, when completed and signed, may give the Health Care provider the authority to withhold or discontinue life-sustaining treatment if that is your expressed desire. The Health Care Power of Attorney, on the other hand, allows you to name someone to act as your agent to make Health Care decisions for you if you cannot. In other words, the agent under the Health Care Power of Attorney only acts when you are incapacitated.

Sometimes there is a discrepancy between what the Living Will says and what the agent under the Health Care Power of Attorney says. It is good to include language in the documents directing whether the agent or the Living Will instruction will have precedence. In some cases, my clients tell me they believe their chosen agent may not have the "guts" to pull the plug, so they want the Living Will to prevail. Others say they would rather the agent consider the situation and deviate from the instructions in the Living Will if the agent believes that is appropriate.

Both the Health Care Power of Attorney and the Living Will are legal documents. Both documents must comply with certain formalities and legal requirements described in the statutes. The documents are state-specific, although most states, including Arizona, have provisions to accept such documents from other states. These documents can be, and sometimes are, challenged in court. Occasionally, for example, there is a dispute among family members as to the proper medical care or the wishes of the person now unable to express himself. Also, if two or more people are named as agents, a disagreement can result in having to go to court to settle the matter.

In Arizona, the agent under the Health Care Power of Attorney is required to engage "substituted judgment" in making decisions on behalf of the incapacitated person. In other words, the agent must make every attempt to be sure the decisions she is making for the incapacitated person are decisions the incapacitated person would make himself if he could. Thus, the agent does not base decisions on what she would choose for herself, nor upon what she feels is in the best interest of the incapacitated person or his family, but only upon what she knows the incapacitated person would want. The agent, therefore, needs to know what the incapacitated person would decide for their own health care if they were able.

This is why I say the documents are not enough. The person signing the documents should have a conversation with the proposed agents and successor agents. Actually, it is probably better to have a series of conversations, especially because things change over time. For many, the conversation is not easy. I remember attempting to have a conversation with my father about his end-of-life wishes. He refused. "That's morbid," he said. At the time, I didn't have a good response.

Now, however, there is a growing movement to have that conversation. The Conversation Project is an organization dedicated to helping people discuss end of life wishes with their loved ones. The Conversation Project has an excellent website (theconversationproject.org.) with a wide variety of resources related to having that discussion. The website includes a course on initiating the conversation, and even includes a starter kit with a workbook-like section to stimulate thoughts about types of decisions that may need to be made.

One reason the conversation is so necessary is it can serve to avoid disputes which sometimes lead to litigation. If loved ones and family members are aware of what someone wants, they are likely to feel more comfortable with decisions made that are consistent with those wishes. It is often uncertainty that leads to a court battle. I sometimes see a family member file in court to become a guardian in order to remove the person named agent under the Health Care Power of Attorney because they disagree with a decision made. Sometimes this is simply a matter of misunderstanding what the incapacitated person really wanted.

While the Conversation Project focuses on talking about health care decisions, I suggest the conversation go beyond that. I strongly believe it is just as important to address wishes regarding after death organ donation, funeral or memorial service, cremation and burial, and the legacy you want to leave behind.

Having the documents Health Care Power of Attorney and Living Will is important. Having the conversation is equally, and probably more, important. Many people have difficulty talking about death. Sometimes it is the parent who has the problem (as in my case) and sometimes it is the child. Using tools such as those on the Conversation Project website can be helpful. Often a family physician or a family attorney can be helpful with the process. Some people may feel more comfortable writing everything down rather than talking out loud. Whatever the method, speaking of death can help assure your wishes are carried out and can often prevent many heartaches for your survivors.

15

MURDER BY DOCUMENT

The Health Care Power of Attorney document is a seemingly simple and benign instrument. But it is actually a powerful document that should be created and used with caution. An interesting example of the power of this document is noted in the reported case of William Van Note. Mind you, this is information that has been provided by various journalists, not court reports, and thus is of questionable reliability. Regardless, the case is instructive.

Mr. Van Note was a 67 year old accountant who had assets of approximately 8 million dollars. In October 2010, he and his fiancé had been together for 20 years and decided to marry. By that time, however, Mr. Van Note had already changed his estate plan to provide for his future wife.

Mr. Van Note's daughter, and would-be sole heir, Susan Elizabeth Van Note, was an attorney in Kansas City who ironically practiced in the area of estate planning and elder law. Her practice, however, did not seem to be going well, as she had filed for bankruptcy in 2009. Susan is now accused of shooting her father and his girlfriend on October 2, 2010. The girlfriend died at the scene, but Mr. Van Note was taken to the hospital and remained in a coma, dependent on a ventilator.

With the girlfriend dead, Susan was the sole heir. She visited her father in the hospital two days after the shooting. She brought with her a

Health Care Power of Attorney, naming her as agent, and giving her the authority to express her father's wishes. Those wishes, according to Susan, were to be disconnected from life support. That was done, and her father died four days after the shooting.

In September 2012, Susan was indicted for first-degree murder for shooting her father and forging the Health Care Power of Attorney document. Another couple has also been charged with providing witness signatures on the allegedly forged documents. The prosecutor has said it was the forgery that resulted in the death of William Van Note: murder by document.

Susan served as Personal Representative (PR) for two years before she was indicted for the murder and removed as PR. She may have used money from the estate to bail herself out of jail.

A year later, in September 2013, Ms. Van Note was charged with the girlfriend's death, as well. The case has been winding through the legal system with components in criminal court and in probate court. The murder trial was scheduled for June and then August 2015, but has been postponed. At the time of publication, the trial is set for February 2017.

If convicted of killing her father, Ms. Van Note will be precluded from receiving her inheritance under Missouri's slayer statute. Missouri, like most states, has a law that prevents someone from benefiting from a death they cause by receiving an inheritance. In fact, a conviction may not be necessary to prove to the Probate Court that Susan should be disinherited. The case is intriguing from both a probate and a criminal point of view.

This case is significant in that it demonstrates the power and the seriousness of a Health Care Power of Attorney. It also demonstrates how the document can be misused and abused. It is actually surprising to me that more providers are not more suspicious of these documents. Most, and probably all, states do have a statute that protects healthcare providers from criminal and civil liability if they follow an advance directive in good faith. So if someone like Ms. Van Note did forge a document (as she is accused of doing), and the hospital did follow her directions (as they did), and what the hospital did was against what the patient really wanted (and maybe it was – we don't really know for sure), the hospital will not be legally liable if they had a good faith basis to believe the document was authentic and valid. That appears to be the case here.

We certainly don't know what really happened in this case. Susan Van Note may be innocent. The Health Care Power of Attorney may have been valid. But the possibility of something like this can happen is very real and is something to think about. Maybe health care providers will be reluctant to accept documents in some circumstances. Maybe family members will challenge documents. At any rate, the documents can be powerful indeed and warrant having them done carefully and properly.

16

GUARDIANSHIPS & CONSERVATORSHIPS

One of the most common legal issues affecting families with a senior, or a family member who has a disability or is incapacitated, is whether or not to establish a guardianship or conservatorship, or both. Below is a basic narrative of terms and the basic process you should know when having to make such a decision. Again, this is a very state specific process. We use Arizona law as an example that is similar to the process of many other states.

In Arizona, a guardian is the person appointed by the court to make medical decisions, placement decisions and lifestyle decisions for an incapacitated person or a minor. On the other hand, a conservator in Arizona manages the assets of someone and makes financial decisions. While the court must find a person to be incapacitated for a guardianship, a conservatorship only needs a showing the person is in need of protection because they are likely to waste or lose assets for whatever reason, and cannot take proper protective measures themselves. The person subject to a guardianship is called a ward, while the person subject to conservatorship is usually known as a protected person.

In some states, the terms used for these same roles are different. For example, in California, the term guardianship only pertains to minors. The court-appointed person who manages medical, food, clothing, shelter, and education decisions for a minor is the "guardian of the person." If managing the assets of a minor, that person is the "guardian of the estate." For adults, California uses the terms, "conservator of the person" and "conservator of the estate."

In Arizona, and in most states, a guardian does the following:

> The guardian is responsible for the care, comfort and maintenance of the ward. The guardian must start conservatorship proceedings if property of the ward is in need of protection.
>
> A guardian is required to report at least annually to the court upon the condition of the ward. The court provides a form for this purpose. A physician's statement is also required every year.
>
> A guardian is required to find the least restrictive setting for his ward, consistent with the ward's needs, capabilities and financial ability, and consistent with the threat, if any, that the ward poses to public safety.
>
> A guardian is required to secure appropriate medical, psychiatric and psychological care and social services.
>
> For involuntary mental health treatment and hospitalization in a locked psychiatric hospital or a psychiatric ward in a general hospital, special additional petitions will be required within the guardianship framework. Such powers can be included or added to a Guardianship.
>
> Guardians may hire case managers, tax preparers, accountants, and bill payers, provided that the guardian oversees them.

Conservator:

In Arizona, the conservator protects and manages the assets belonging to a protected person. The conservator must file an inventory of the protected person's property, and a budget within 90 days of appointment, file an annual accounting and protect the person's assets. The conservator must avoid conflicts of interest and self-dealing.

The general process in Arizona to appoint a Guardian or Conservator includes the following:

> Petition for appointment of Guardian or Conservator or both. This is the request to the court that has some basic information about why the appointment is necessary and why the person requesting should be appointed.
> Petition for Appointment of Attorney, Medical Examiner, and Investigator. The court must appoint both an attorney for the ward and an investigator. The attorney for the ward is required to visit the ward and to represent what the ward wants. If, for example, the ward wants to object to the guardianship or to the particular person seeking to be guardian, the ward's attorney will object and will represent the ward at the contested hearing. The court investigator will visit the ward, talk to anyone involved, and make a recommendation to the court as to whether a guardianship is needed and whether the person requesting to be guardian is appropriate. The medical examiner, on the other hand, is most often the ward's health care provider and is required to complete a form indicating whether the ward needs a guardian.
> Notify Attorney, Medical Examiner and Investigator that they have been appointed. The petitioner is charged with the responsibility of notifying any player of the proceeding. Notify relatives of the pendency of the action. In Arizona, it is necessary to notify adult children and parents. Specific rules apply to how people are notified.
> Schedule the hearing on Guardianship or Conservatorship. The court will set a hearing date and the petitioner will include that date with notifications.
> Obtain the medical report from the Medical Examiner for Guardianship cases and distribute it.

Apply for appropriate bond in a conservatorship case.

If the case is not contested, prepare an order for the Judge to sign and present evidence at the non-contested evidentiary hearing.

Once the order is signed, file the bond (conservatorship) and get the Clerk of the Court to issue "Letters." "Letters" of Guardianship and/or Conservatorship is usually a one page document signed by the Probate Clerk. This is the document used to show the guardian or conservator has been appointed and has authority.

File a conservatorship inventory and budget within the specified time.

Many petitioners use an attorney to represent them in this process. It is, however, possible to get a guardian or conservator appointed without one. The process is very form-intensive and tedious. In many jurisdictions forms are available online or at the courthouse. Sometimes help is available through the local Legal Aid office. Some attorneys will take these cases on a limited-representation basis to help save money. Such representation may include reviewing paperwork prepared and filed by the client. Sometimes, the representation includes just court appearances. Limited-representation is not available in every jurisdiction or from every attorney.

The process of guardianship and conservatorship will usually take anywhere from 30-45 days in most jurisdictions. Contested cases can take several months before someone is appointed. As you can imagine, though, the situation can constitute an emergency. There is a process for appointing a temporary Guardian or Conservator in the case of a real emergency, which can take only about 24 to 48 hours. The emergency must generally constitute a clear and present threat to the Ward's health or an immediate threat that his finances will be wasted or dissipated unless a Guardian or Conservator is appointed.

17

PROPERTY & CASUALTY INSURANCE

I want to address issues of homeowners and automobile insurance. These areas are often overlooked when dealing with estate planning issues. Insurance is the first line of defense and is important to protect assets that go far beyond the home and the auto.

Homeowners Insurance
As with any insurance, it is good to read your policy. Most never do, until there is a problem with a claim. At the very least, be familiar with your declaration page – the page listing the amounts of your coverage in each category.

Homeowners insurance generally covers the dwelling, personal property, loss of use, and liability. For the coverage on the house itself, and anything inside, most people want "replacement cost." Many policies will cover "market value" or "cash value" unless you have specifically asked for and paid for replacement cost. Check and see how your company defines replacement cost, as there may be variations. Cash value coverage will apply depreciation, which often will result in payment by your insurance company of far less than what you can replace your property for. Inform your agent or company of any remodeling, additions, or any other improvements that increase the value of the property and make sure your limits are increased accordingly.

The contents of your house, your personal property, are often covered at a fixed amount or a percentage of the dwelling coverage. Be sure that your insurance agent or company is aware of any particular item that would need to be separately listed, like valuable artwork or jewelry. Keep good records and photographs. Items can be scheduled and covered individually, which is a good idea. This is also a good way to keep records for the rest of your estate planning.

Your insurance should also provide coverage for "loss of use" or living expenses if you are not able to remain in the home. Sometimes this is referred to as Additional Living Expenses (ALE). This can cover all or a portion of hotel expenses and meals. Usually, the maximum amount of the coverage is a percentage of your insurance on your home.

It usually makes sense to have as high a deductible as you can afford. The savings in premium is usually worth it. And insurance coverage is just as important if you are renting. Renters' policies can cover contents and liability.

The liability portion of your insurance coverage is extremely important. This is one way you can protect your assets. Liability insurance may cover someone's injuries that occur on your property and even off the property, but for which you are liable. This can obviously be very valuable coverage. If, for example, someone is injured on your property and you are found liable, that person may be awarded a large amount of money. Your liability coverage can pay for that, protecting your other assets – money in the bank, investment accounts, and even your income. Note, however, certain acts may be excluded and not covered at all. Check the exclusions section of the policy.

For most people who have a mortgage, the mortgage company is either paying the homeowner's insurance premium from an escrow account, or verifying that is being paid. Once the home is paid for, the homeowner is responsible for keeping up with the homeowners' insurance premium payments. Automatic payments from the same account as the one with direct deposit is always a good idea.

Automobile Insurance

Arizona, like other states, requires minimum limits of liability insurance. A vehicle owner can, however, waive the insurance requirement by self-insuring. In order to self-insure, you must assign a Certificate of Deposit of $40,000 to the Office of the Arizona State treasurer. I strongly recommend you not waive coverage and strongly recommend you purchase far more than the minimum liability coverage. The minimums will pay $15,000 per person and up to $30,000 per accident for bodily injury. That will not go very far. Minimum property damage is only $10,000 – not enough to cover most vehicles on the road today. If your liability coverage is less than six figures, it is probably too low.

But the liability portion only covers injury and damage to someone else. Coverage for damage to your vehicle is called collision for accidents and comprehensive for other types of damage or loss (weather, theft, etc.). These are coverages to which a deductible usually applies.

People may refer to the above types of auto coverage as "full coverage" which means you have required liability plus some insurance on your vehicle, as well. This may be called full coverage, but it has several gaps. The limits must be adequate – in my opinion, adequate is far higher than minimum. And several other coverages are also necessary.

Many other types of coverage are extremely important. One such coverage is "Medical Payments" coverage that will pay a few thousand in medical bills for your injuries from an accident, no matter who is at fault. Med Pay can pay your health care deductibles, co-pay, physical therapy, chiropractor, and most other costs.

Also very important is "Uninsured" and "Underinsured" coverage. These will protect you and your passengers for bodily injuries when the other driver is at fault and does not have any, or enough, coverage to compensate those injuries. For example, if the 18 year old who ran into you had minimum liability coverage of $15,000 (again, the amount of required minimum liability insurance in Arizona – other states vary), and your injuries (or passengers) far exceeded that, your uninsured and underinsured coverage will pay the difference. These limits should also be as high as you can afford. The costs are relatively low and Arizona is a state with very high rates of uninsured and underinsured drivers.

Medical payment coverage, uninsured, and underinsured are very important, especially if you are on a fixed income and may have deductibles and co-insurance to worry about. Imagine needing surgery, a long period of physical therapy, or prolonged rehabilitation as a result of an accident. Even if you are told you have full coverage, these coverages are not necessarily included.

Personal Umbrella Policy

Lastly, I want to mention the relatively inexpensive liability coverage of a Personal Umbrella Policy. These policies basically overlay your other insurance liability coverage. In other words, your umbrella policy will pay, in increments of one million dollars usually, for any liability exceeding the limits on your auto or homeowners policies. You will be required to have specific limits of liability on your underlying auto and homeowner's policy, but the umbrella can give you much added protection, as well.

Obviously, I am a strong believer in insurance, especially for older adults. Why? The answer is simple. Older people are far more likely to require asset protection that many younger people. If I am advising a person in his young 20's, I may determine that person is "judgment proof." That means they have no assets that can be taken away from them. Older people, though, have often worked a lifetime and accumulated some assets. Maybe a house is paid for and greatly appreciated. Maybe there are large amounts of savings, investment accounts, vacation homes, or other things you could lose if you are sued. If you are the party liable for an accident, causing damage or injury your assets will be discovered. Also, catastrophic medical bills can also wipe out your savings. It is imperative to protect what you have worked for.

Some assets such as all or a portion of your home, some or all of income, and certain retirement funds may be protected from judgement creditors by state or federal law. Many assets have no such protection.

Of course, there are older people who are "judgment proof." These are people who have no savings, no investments, no real estate, except their personal residence, and live on social security. In other words, they are "judgment proof" because they have no assets to go after. Many of your assets may be protected in an irrevocable trust or a protected type of account such as an IRA or 401K. This is one of those areas where you should consult with an attorney who knows and understands this type of law.

18

DO YOU HAVE AN ESTAE PLAN FOR YOUR FACEBOOK ACCOUNT (AND OTHER DIGITAL ASSETS)

In response to many of their account holder's families, Facebook implemented a feature that allows users to designate what Facebook calls a Legacy Contact for their Facebook accounts. What this means is you can now directly let Facebook know who will be in control of your account after you die. It is a way, also, to turn your Timeline into a memorial. In addition, you can let Facebook know if you want your account to be permanently deleted after your death just by adjusting your account settings.

There are clear parameters in place so that a Legacy Contact isn't allowed to take over a deceased user's Facebook account and continue to use it as if the person were still alive. A Legacy Contact will have access to the Facebook Account but will be only allowed to do the following with the deceased user's account:

> Write a post to display at the top of the memorialized Timeline
> Respond to new friend requests for the memorialized profile
> Update the profile picture and cover photo

Download an archive of the photos, posts and profile information shared on Facebook- only if you elected to do so

Don't be concerned that the person chosen as your Legacy Contact will be able to log in as you. Facebook has made provisions to prevent that, as well as making sure that they will not be able to read your private messages.

And your Legacy Contact will not have access to your account until after Facebook is notified of your death. A friend or family member can notify Facebook of your death. Proof, such as an obituary or death certificate, can accompany the notification, but is not required.

So how do you designate your Legacy Contact? Facebook users only need to open their Settings, then open their security options, and designate their Legacy Contact. You can opt to send a message to that person, which would be highly recommended. You will also be able to give permission for your Legacy Contact to download an archived version of your Facebook posts, photos and profile information. You can find more information on Facebook's help site.

You can, and should, also mention your Legacy Contact in your will or other estate planning documents. Facebook indicates it "may" provide information, presumably the same information and access provided to a designated Legacy Contact, to a person indicated in your will or another legal document granting consent. The Legacy Contact, however, is only helpful in the event of death and not for other forms of disability or incapacity.

While Facebook has been proactive in the area of providing users with a way to plan for their accounts after death, many other providers have not. And most people now have a growing number of what we are calling digital assets. All of these should be included in your estate planning to help manage your online accounts when you no longer can. Such a plan can, and should, be a part of your will, Living Trust, and financial power of attorney, and information should be conveyed to the individuals who will be in charge of the digital portions of your estate.

For example, people have websites, or data stored on other websites, social media profiles, photographs, music libraries, emails, PDF documents, files, and a variety of web-based businesses, including E-bay storefronts and PayPal accounts. Also, many people have blogs or websites, along with a spectrum of affiliate accounts with various vendors and advertising contracts. These are not provided for in a traditional estate plan. In fact, people need a way to "protect" all of their password-protected information as part of their estate plan.

In the "olden" days, when someone died, the most effective way for their personal representative (executor) or successor trustee to identify all of their accounts, debts, and financial information, was to take control of their mail. The mail is forwarded to the personal representative (executor) or to the attorney and within a month or two (three at the most for quarterly statements) all of the important information was discovered. Now, however, many have gone paperless and all of their statements go to their email, and many of their transactions occur online. The executor or successor trustee is often locked out of those sites.

To make things worse, companies often have very restrictive terms of service that address access to the information, and legislation such as the Stored Communications Act of 1986 further restricts disclosure by the company.

In 2014, the Uniform Fiduciary Access to Digital Assets Act (UFADAA) was drafted. This proposed legislation is available for states to enact to deal with managing digital assets in the event of death or disability. The act would provide access to executors (personal representatives) of estates, agents under powers of attorney, trustees and successor trustees, and court-appointed guardians and conservators. It will override certain provisions in terms of service agreements, if those provisions conflict with express instructions of the account holder. Instructions can be conveyed through a will, trust, and/or power of attorney. As of mid-2016, the act has been introduced in 26 states, but has been enacted in just a few, including Arizona.

Basic estate planning for digital assets can include:

Maintain a list of all accounts and passwords. This list is kept in a safe place – if paper, locked in a safety deposit box or other safe. Make sure someone else has access to the storage place. The list can also be digital with a separate password provided to a trusted individual.

Refer to the list in your will or trust (or both). Do not include the actual list or any passwords in the will as this can become public. Although trusts are designed to be private, passwords should not be listed there, either.

Include clauses in your trust granting authorization to the successor trustee to access your accounts and account information. The same authority should be included in the will for the executor, but a will generally requires court action to give the executor authority. Update the information as necessary.

This is an area of law that is sure to continue evolving over the next several years. The digital age is just beginning and I am sure there are aspects that will need to be considered, but we have not even conceived of. This is yet another reason to have and maintain a relationship with an attorney who is active and current in the field of estate planning.

19

PROTECTING YOUR PET

I often say that my dear cat, Lillie, had never disappointed me. Many people feel the same way about their pet. We should also be careful not to disappoint our pet. Think about what would happen to your pet if you didn't come home one day? What would happen if you were in an accident, fell seriously ill, or that eventual day when you won't ever come home to your pet again? The prospect of your pet outliving you must be considered as part of your estate planning.

Yes, our pets are very special. In the United States, over 71 million households own a pet. Many own more than one pet. Surveys reveal people are extremely close to their animals, with 79% admitting they sleep with their pet and 31% admitting they have taken time off work to be with a sick pet. One source reported that 70% responded if stranded on a desert isle, they would rather be with a pet than a spouse. This may explain why more than 40 billion dollars are spent on pets.

It is only natural people take steps to protect their pet in the event they become disabled, incapacitated, or die. You can also protect against the other "d" word – divorce. Some married couples have entered into an agreement, sometimes known as a pet-nup, to provide for pet issues upon divorce. Language can also be included in a standard pre-nuptial agreement to address issues such as custody, visitation, health decisions, and maintenance of a pet upon divorce.

For the protection and well being of their pets, there are a number of common sense measures I suggest clients take. One such measure is to carry a pet emergency alert card in your wallet. The pet card provides information that a pet is at your home, and a list of emergency caregivers for the pet. The card will alert emergency personnel of the pet's existence in the event you are hospitalized or dead. There have been many cases of pets dying from neglect when the owner is in an accident or killed and people are unaware there is a pet waiting at home. In fact, this was a very sad occurrence in the aftermath of the terrorist attack on September 11, 2001.

Pet owners should also have a door sign at their home alerting emergency workers to pets inside. If something happens such as a mechanical problem, gas leak, flood, break-in, or fire, and emergency workers must enter, they will be aware of the pets and be able to take measures to rescue or protect the pets. It is also a courtesy notice to emergency workers if the pet is protective of the residence. In addition, you should have some form of pet document describing the animal, emergency contacts, pet sitter, kennel, veterinarian, and any other information pertinent to your pet (medical issues, medications, etc.). This document should be kept in the house where it will likely be found – near pet food, on the refrigerator, and a copy with your estate planning documents, such as your will and trust and powers of attorney.

It is also important to include specific language regarding your pet in your Durable Power of Attorney (the financial power), or to have a limited separate power of attorney form for your pet(s). This should include granting your agent or attorney-in-fact power to consent to any type of veterinary care, and performing any act related to the care, maintenance, feeding, supervision, safety and welfare of the pet(s).

The animal card, sign, document and power of attorney are for the short term. These are important to cover emergencies, disasters, and periods of absence, disability, or incapacity. For the longer-term, in other words, if your pet outlives you, then you must consider providing for the pet in your will or trust.

In your will, you can create a testamentary trust to provide for your pet. Because pets are considered personal property, you can also devise (leave) your pet to a particular individual. In some cases, I have seen a person leave the pet and a set amount of money for the care of the pet, to an individual. The problem with this approach is without a trust, there is no way to make sure the person keeps the pet or uses the money for the pet. Also, this method would not provide for what happens to the pet if the pet's new owner became incapacitated or did not outlive the animal. It may or may not work.

One of the best ways to plan for a pet is with a pet trust. A trust can identify a trustee to administer the property in the trust – namely the pet (because pets are considered personal property) and the amount of money designated for the care of the pet. The trustee would dispense funds to the beneficiary (caregiver) who is given custody of the pet. The trust should name alternates and successors for both trustee and beneficiary. The trust can also describe the type of lifestyle you'd like the pet to have – exercise program, types of food, contact with others, living conditions, etc. You can also specify methods for monitoring the care of the pet and making sure the caregiver is following the instructions. Often, the monitor is the trustee. There also needs to be a remainder beneficiary. The remainder beneficiary is the person to whom the remaining assets in the trust would go when the pet dies.

In Arizona, as in many states, we have a statutory pet trust providing a lot of the detail. A.R.S. 14-2907 and 14-10408 provides for trusts for animals and limits their duration to the lifetime of the animal. Under these statutes, any money in the trust can only be used for the animal or pet and if no trustee is named, the court will name one. The court can also fill in other gaps, while maintaining the trust for the benefit of the pet.

Many people are unaware an estate plan can, and often should, include pets. This is an important area to explore with the attorney helping with the plan. Many attorneys now routinely ask about pets when gathering family information. If not, be sure to raise the issue and include those non-human best friends. After all, your pet has never disappointed you and you should not disappoint your pet.

20

CHOOSING YOUR SUCCESSOR TRUSTEE, EXECUTOR OR AGENT

People often struggle with the decision of who should be placed in positions of authority in their estate planning documents. In fact, not knowing who to choose for these key roles is one reason people often put off their estate planning. There are three or four major roles that must be filled as part of your estate plan. Each of these roles gives individuals or entities a great deal of power and responsibility over your person and/or your estate. The major positions are successor trustee, personal representative, financial power of attorney, and health care agent. A successor trustee is needed if you have a trust. Any type of estate plan requires powers of attorney and a personal representative, trust or not. Everyone should have a health care agent.

If you have a Revocable Living Trust (RLT), it is most likely you will act as your own trustee unless and until you become incapacitated, or when you die. If you are married, you will probably be co-trustee with your spouse. As trustee, you have full authority over your assets while you are alive and well. Upon your incapacity or death, if there is a spouse serving as co-trustee, that person may be designated to serve alone until their death or incapacity. A decision must be made, however, who will eventually serve as the successor trustee. That person will have the responsibility to manage your assets according to the directions you included in your trust. Duties include paying your expenses, maintaining your property, providing for your care if you are incapacitated, and distributing your assets to others after your death.

The personal representative is the person who administers your will after your death. In some states this person is called executor. He or she will administer and settle your estate, performing the same types of duties as a successor trustee performs after your death. If you have both a will and a trust, the goal is that the will may not be necessary and the trustee is able to settle the estate without probate. If probate is needed, however, the personal representative will have to act. Even though you name a Personal Representative in your will, that person has no power unless and until appointed by the court. In most cases, a probate action must be filed in court in order for a personal representative to be able to act in that role.

The agent under your financial power of attorney (FPOA) is often referred to as your "attorney-in-fact." This person or entity has the authority to manage your assets while you are alive. The authority under this power of attorney ends when you die. It is most useful if you are incapacitated and need someone to be in charge of finances, but can also be written to allow someone to engage in financial transactions on your behalf even if you are not incapacitated. If you also have a trust, your FPOA only has authority over property not titled in the name of your trust. The trustee or successor trustee controls anything in the trust.

The successor trustee, personal representative, and attorney-in-fact (financial power of attorney) all serve as fiduciaries and must be extremely careful to appropriately handle your finances. Very often, these three positions are held by the same individual or entity. Strict laws govern what they can and cannot do, along with the instructions in your documents. The rule of thumb is they must make sure all your assets are used for your benefit unless you have specifically provided otherwise in writing. I have seen many people in these positions end up in court because they engaged in self-dealing or otherwise violated the strict requirements of the law. Often these violations are innocent and even inadvertent, but can still result in serious penalties.

The health care agent serves in a very different role. This person is responsible for making decisions about your person, basically medical and placement decisions, when you cannot. Therefore, it is important the agent know what your wishes are in regard to your care and treatment. Often, the successor trustee, personal representative, and attorney-in-fact are the same person, while the health care agent is someone else.

Many people choose their children or another relative for all of these roles. This is often not a good idea. A colleague of mine says, "The only thing worse than naming your child as successor trustee, is naming two children as successor trustee." What he is trying to convey is that problems sometimes arise when a family member, especially a child, is placed in that role.

I think it is sometimes appropriate to name a family member, even an adult child. I agree, however, that it is almost always a bad idea to name two or more children as successor co-trustees, or co-agents on a power of attorney. Although legally permissible, naming two people is often an invitation for problems.

In many cases, I recommend hiring a professional as a successor trustee, and even as a personal representative and financial power of attorney (attorney-in-fact). Often, a family member or close friend is a good choice for health care agent, but on rare occasions, a professional should be used for that position as well. Every situation is different.

Where do you find a professional? Some people ask their CPA or attorney. Not all CPAs and attorneys will serve in those roles, but some will. Otherwise, they may be able to refer to an appropriate person or entity. Sometimes a financial advisor will serve. In Arizona, and in many other states, there are licensed or certified fiduciaries who have received training to serve in these fiduciary positions. There are numerous Trust companies available to meet the wide variety of needs.

When choosing a professional to act as fiduciary, consider factors such as fees and specific duties performed. Some may charge a percentage, while others charge by the hour. Some charge separately to manage investments. The charges of most of these professionals will be far less than the cost of litigation, mismanagement, and other forms of waste that often occurs with inexperienced fiduciaries. In most cases, hiring a professional to administer the trust or estate is money well spent. These decisions are some of the things an experienced estate planning attorney will be helping with as you design your estate plan.

21

THE PERILS OF BEING A TRUSTEE, EXCUTOR OR AGENT

What if you find yourself acting as someone's agent under a financial power of attorney? Or if you assume the responsibilities as a personal representative (executor) or as a successor trustee? In all three of these roles, you have fiduciary duties prescribed by the law. You can now be exposed to serious penalties for breaching those duties. Although I rarely see the penalties invoked, for a variety of reasons, I do often see large amounts of money expended in legal fees defending or prosecuting breaches of fiduciary duties. This chapter will address the duties that apply to all three of these roles – agent under a power of attorney, personal representative in a will, or successor trustee of a trust.

Many of the requirements are counter-intuitive. It is easy to violate the law regarding fiduciaryduties, while trying very hard to carry out the intent of the person who appointed you. But sometimes what they intended just doesn't matter. Intent must be expressed in the proper way, and all too frequently, it is not.

What is a fiduciary? A fiduciary is someone who is in a position of trust and confidence to someone else, usually in regard to taking care of money for that other person. This relationship is considered to require the highest legal and ethical standard of care. A fiduciary responsibility exists between a trustee and a beneficiary of a trust, and between an agent and principal of a power of attorney. The principal is the person who appointed the agent. The personal representative, also known as the executor, of an estate may have a fiduciary duty to devisees and legatees (people who receive property under a will), heirs (people who would inherit if there was no will), and creditors. Guardians and conservators are also fiduciaries.

Some people are specifically referred to as fiduciary in their title. Many states license or certify private fiduciaries who can serve in roles such as agent under a power of attorney, personal representative, or trustee, and charge a fee for their service. These individuals and firms often act in that capacity for estates, in the same way a trust company or bank will sometimes serve as a trustee. All have a fiduciary relationship and must fulfill fiduciary duties. Fiduciary duties, whatever the role, include a duty of loyalty, duty of care, duty of impartiality, and prudent administration.

Most jurisdictions also have a public fiduciary who is often assigned to take over and control assets of someone who is incapacitated or in need of protection and has no one else to serve in that role. Often these public fiduciaries have a number of other roles they play, often settling estates of individuals when no one else is available, and assisting with disposing assets of indigent people and making their final arrangements. The public fiduciary is usually considered the fiduciary of last resort.

A good rule of thumb for the fiduciary is to avoid doing anything to benefit themselves or a family member, other than the person for whom they are fiduciary. With a power of attorney, the agent is often entrusted with financial assets. These assets do not belong to the agent and can only be used for the benefit of the principal. Exceptions to this rule are the court can approve a deviation, or the principal can authorize a deviation. That authorization, however, should be within the document or otherwise in writing. The principal may, for example, include a gifting provision in the power of attorney document and indicate the agent may make gifts to himself. In some cases, the agent can make gifts to others, but not himself, and in other cases can make no gifts at all. These distinctions must be made within the power of attorney document.

A fiduciary who is named in any role such as agent under a power of attorney, personal representative in a will, or as a successor trustee, may or may not be entitled to payment for their services. The document will often specify that the fiduciary can be paid a reasonable amount, or sometimes a fixed fee. Sometimes, I see documents indicate a fiduciary is to be paid only if they are not related to the person naming them, or, if they are not a beneficiary. Some documents indicate no one can be compensated for their work. If the document does not address compensation at all, the law may allow reasonable compensation for services and reimbursement for expenses. The work may be considerable, and the responsibilities are huge. Many people will decline the job if they are not compensated for their time. Of course, if choosing an institution like a trust company or a professional fiduciary, they will be paid or probably decline the job.

Sometimes, when the appointed fiduciary is a friend or relative, duties and responsibilities may be influenced by the knowledge the fiduciary has of the person for whom they are fiduciary. This can result in an inadvertent and even an innocent breach. For example, someone is appointed agent under a power of attorney for a parent who is incapacitated, and the incapacitated person can no longer drive. In the past the principal had told the agent, and others that he wanted to give the car to the person named as agent. If the agent uses the power of attorney to transfer the vehicle to himself, and the document does not specifically authorize that gift, this would be a breach of fiduciary duty. Agents must be extremely careful not to use the power of attorney to transfer property to themselves, even if just for convenience.

Sometimes, when the principal is incapacitated and very ill at the end of life, the agent will begin moving assets in anticipation of death. Don't do it. In one of my cases, the client was agent under a power of attorney for her grandfather. The principal (grandfather) was on hospice and his death was imminent. He had an estate plan leaving everything to his granddaughter – the same person who was the agent. In the weeks before his death, the granddaughter, as agent, began writing checks to herself and other family members thinking it would be easier and would avoid hassles after his death. This action on the part of the agent was a breach of her fiduciary duties and was challenged by other relatives. Those relatives hoped she would be found to have breached her duties, financially exploited her grandfather, and forced to repay double what she transferred. Those other relatives then would have asked the offending granddaughter be disinherited, allowing everything to pass to the other relatives. The case eventually resolved in favor of my client, but not until tens of thousands of dollars had been spent on legal costs.

In Arizona, such breaches may be interpreted as exploitation of a vulnerable adult, and can result in the serious penalties noted above. Some of those penalties include repaying double the amount taken, paying attorney fees and court costs for the person bringing the action, and even being disinherited. The person who is found to have exploited the vulnerable adult can be precluded from receiving any gift from a will or trust, any life insurance policy, or any other account for which the exploiter was a beneficiary.

Joint accounts also hold conditions to be aware of. This is different from, but related to fiduciary duties and is worth mentioning here. Many people will put a child or another person on their account, as a joint owner, for convenience. First, this is rarely advisable or necessary. Someone can be added to an account as a signer (usually through a power of attorney) and can also be designated as a beneficiary of an account (transfer on death or pay on death) so the account goes to that person after death. If, however, someone is placed on an account as a joint owner, under Arizona law and the law of many other jurisdictions, while both owners are alive the money in that account only belongs to the person in proportion to what they contributed. If your parent has listed you as a joint owner on their account, and you have never deposited any of your money into the account, you cannot use money in that account for your own benefit without the authorization of the other owner. Of course, the financial institution will allow you to make withdrawals and they do not police the accounts. The joint owner of an account will own the account upon the death of the other owner. The argument, "It's going to be mine one day anyway" is not a justification for raiding the account before the other owner dies.

Acting as a fiduciary is a huge responsibility and acting in that capacity can be particularly perilous. A properly drafted document can go a long way in protecting both the principal and fiduciary. It is well worth the expense to meet with an experienced estate planning attorney who will know what questions to ask and what clauses to include in a document to make sure the principal's intent is followed and the agent is able to act in a manner most consistent with what the principal wanted. As always, proper planning can often prevent damaged relationships and save a great deal in future legal fees, time, and other expense.

22

PLANNING ON A SHOESTRING

Legal fees are expensive. In fact, the cost of legal services can be prohibitively expensive. That fact leads people to deceptively inexpensive alternatives such as do-it-yourself forms or using online discount products. Unfortunately, as I have pointed out, cutting corners often leads to even higher legal fees as incomplete or vague estate planning can lead to even more expensive litigation. All too often, the inexpensive, corner-cutting alternatives do not consider distinctions in local law and nuances that can make big differences. In estate planning particularly, one-size-fits-all plans often lead to frightening and expensive unintended consequences.

I have often seen people with do-it-yourself or online wills and trusts which simply did not work the way it was hoped or intended. Recently, I had a client whose father had done a trust many years ago. He hired an attorney to do the work and that same attorney amended the trust a couple times. Shortly before his death, the Trustmaker (also referred to as grantor, trustor, or settlor) created another amendment. His son (my client) told me his father had said, "I'm not paying that attorney again for something I can do myself." He followed the format of previous amendments and drafted language giving certain property to the son and attempting to exclude other beneficiaries. Unfortunately, the language was vague and it was difficult to determine exactly what was included. He saved a few hundred dollars for the cost of the amendment, but the cost of litigation after his death cost far exceeded what he saved. The court needed to intervene to interpret what he intended and even replaced the family-member successor trustees the Trustmaker had chosen with an independent fiduciary. In addition to the financial cost, family relationships were probably permanently damaged.

I tell people even if they attempt estate planning documents on their own, they should hire an attorney to review them. Pay for an hour of an attorney's time. Ask the attorney's opinion on how the documents will work. Ask for suggested changes. This may cost between $150 and $300 or slightly more, but can potentially save tens of thousands. Also, it can help assure your wishes will be followed and the documents may either avoid court or hold up in court.

Some attorneys offer a free consultation. I don't. My philosophy is that if you come to see me, I am going to make sure you leave with valuable information. I generally charge a flat rate and make myself available for one to two hours for a typical estate planning consultation. If you are asking me to review documents, and they are not voluminous, I will review them during that meeting. Sometimes, I will draft a document or two in that same meeting. If the consult is for establishing a new plan, we will usually discuss the pros and cons of different plans – trust vs. will, etc. Whatever the purpose of the visit, you should leave with a firm understanding of your needs, options, alternatives, and potential costs.

For some of the other types of cases such as will contests, trust disputes, and contested guardianships, I will evaluate the case at the consultation. I will explain the applicable law and apply your facts. Together, we will explore any non-litigation approaches, evaluate the options, alternatives, and likelihood of success. I will either advise you not to pursue the case, advise you to go forward on your own, or I may offer to represent you or even refer you to a more appropriate legal representative.

I've had people tell me they don't want to come in for a consultation unless I assure them I will take the case. I cannot, however, know if I can take the case unless I learn about the case. The initial consultation is a time for the attorney and prospective client to get together and see if they are a good fit and if the attorney's knowledge and experience are appropriate for this case. The client should receive an honest assessment of their case and as accurate as possible description of potential costs. At times, I determine I am not the best choice of attorney for the case and client. I will explain how I arrived at that conclusion and I will refer the client somewhere else. If they like, I can even pass along information to another attorney, including my thoughts on the case and the needs of the client.

There can be great value in even an initial consultation with an attorney or an hour meeting to review documents and ask questions. Much can depend on preparation for the appointment. If the purpose is to have documents reviewed, to determine if changes are needed, bring all the documents or send them ahead of time. It is usually better to bring more than less. Let the attorney decide what he or she needs.

Some attorneys have lists and worksheets to fill out ahead of an appointment. Sometimes this works well to prepare for the appointment. More often than not, I prefer to ask questions and listen to what the prospective client is saying. I usually take detailed notes and often ask the client to gather additional information. Everybody's style is different. In this information age, a great deal of material is available online. I am finding more and more clients are doing extensive research prior to meeting with an attorney. That can be a great help, but can also be a hindrance. It is very difficult to get a good balance of information. I do suggest, however, that each prospective client give some thought to what they want from their visit and write down questions or topics to address.

Seeing an attorney doesn't necessarily mean you are buying a long and expensive relationship. Hopefully, your issues can be resolved in a one or two hour appointment. Documents can be reviewed, advice given, and suggestions made. Many attorneys are open to this type of relationship and consumers can often accomplish far more than expected in one or two hours of time with an experienced attorney.

23

LIBRARY FIRES & ETHICAL WILLS

There are actually three types of documents referred to as "wills." First is the will of inheritance, often known as the Last Will and Testament. This will is designed to be effective upon death, and its primary purpose is to direct the final administration of the dead person's estate and the distribution of their property. This will may also name a guardian for minor children and possibly for an incapacitated adult. The second type is the Living Will. The Living Will is usually a statement of what type of care a person wants when they are ill and cannot express their wishes themselves. Most often, it is applicable when the person has a terminal illness, their death is imminent, or they may be in a persistent vegetative state or irreversible coma. If it appears life-sustaining treatment would only prolong the moment of death, the Living Will indicates whether life-sustaining treatment is desired. Usually, life-sustaining treatment is defined, and the definition may include things like artificially administered food and fluid, CPR, mechanical ventilation, dialysis, etc.

The third type of will is the lesser-known Ethical Will. The Ethical Will is a document that is used to communicate values, beliefs, hopes for the future, advice, life lessons, forgiveness, love, and often personal history. While your Last Will and Testament tells people what you want them to have, the Ethical Will tells people what you want them to know. Unlike the other two types of wills, the Ethical Will is not a legal document, but can be of great value and utility, and is useful in preparing the other estate planning legal documents. When properly done, an Ethical Will can make a huge difference for the surviving loved ones.

The concept of Ethical Wills is ancient. The bible, both Old and New Testaments have examples of ethical wills. In Genesis, Jacob's farewell to his children is an Ethical Will, as is Moses' farewell to the children of Israel in Deuteronomy. In the New Testament, Jesus' last words to the disciples, in the book of John, is another example.

In ancient times, Ethical Wills were oral. Later they were written, and today can take many forms. Most often, the Ethical Will is presented in writing, but there are also examples of recorded and video formats, which are becoming more popular. In fact, several videography companies focus on assisting people with videos that will record personal history and life lessons they wish to preserve and pass on to future generations. These are actually Ethical Wills, although they may be called by another name.

Some people will include lessons, values, advice and other components of Ethical Wills within their Last Will and Testament or their Revocable Trust. Some examples of incorporating Ethical Will language into a Last Will and Testament are seen from colonial times in the will of George Washington. Washington wrote a beautiful will describing and explaining his bequests. For example, he left money for establishing a university, explaining his reasoning and his wishes for that institution. He did the same with his bequest of swords to his nephews and telling how he hoped those swords would be treated and used by the recipients. Often, information like this is included in wills and considered precatory. In other words, the instructions may not be legally binding, but convey what the testator hopes would happen.

Today, it is less common to include Ethical Will language within a Last Will and Testament. There is, however, nothing wrong with it. Some estate planning attorneys create trusts that include sections that represent the same things as an Ethical Will. Sometimes, this is called a "purposeful trust" and practitioners who draft them can be located by searching that term on the internet.

Very often, an Ethical Will takes the form of a letter. Some people write a general letter and others write several: one for the spouse, one for each child and special friends. For some, their Ethical Will takes the form of a memoir. It may be a poem. Preparing the document, in whatever form, is an opportunity to not only pass along what you want to convey to others, but also is an opportunity to reflect on the meaning and importance of your life. By creating something that will live on, the person preparing the Ethical Will can view his or her own mortality in a different light. Clients have told me, the thoughts that went into the ethical will clarified many of the questions and struggles they had in drafting a trust or a Last Will and Testament or a Living Will.

Although it is never too early to write an Ethical Will, it can easily become too late. Some are inspired by a change in their health, the death of someone close to them, or a milestone reaching a certain age. Other life events such as a marriage, retirement, or a planned surgery may cause someone to want to record their reflections in an Ethical Will. For some, being placed on hospice is the time they consider writing or recording their personal history, values and life lessons.

Everybody has something to contribute to someone else. Everybody has a story – in fact, everybody has hundreds or thousands of stories. There is a Middle Eastern saying that when an old person dies, it is like a library burning. Their stories die with them, along with their wisdom, life lessons, values, and all they have learned from their unique experiences. These stories, experiences, and lessons can be preserved in an Ethical Will.

Many estate planning attorneys can help direct people to resources to use to compile an Ethical Will or similar document, recording or video. These tools can also be very useful in preparing other parts of the estate plan because the reflection and thought that goes into an Ethical Will often clarifies goals and objectives of the plan. This process can be extremely rewarding and helpful. Don't let your library burn.

24

ESTATE PLANNING MYTHS, MISSTEPS, AND MESS UPS

Over the years, I have encountered a number of situations, after a death, that have resulted in significant expense, aggravation, and frustration, all of which could have been easily avoided. Often these situations arise due to misunderstanding, misinterpretation, and efforts to cut corners on planning in an effort to save money. Here are just a few examples:

1. Inadvertent disinheritance

Sometimes people intend to disinherit a family member for good reason. But sometimes heirs are disinherited unintentionally and there is often no remedy. One way this happens is when someone doesn't quite understand the interaction of probate and non-probate transfers. A probate transfer is property that transfers through a probate estate. A probate estate is transferred through a will or through the state laws known as intestate succession. The will gives instruction on how to divide and distribute property. If there is no will, state law dictates how property is divided and distributed. In either case, the process usually requires court action (probate), in the form of probating a will and/or appointing a personal representative (executor). The personal representative is responsible for gathering, dividing, and distributing assets.

It is important to be aware many distributions occur outside of probate. These do not go through the court process. For example, any property owned jointly with a right of survivorship will pass outside probate to the survivor. This often happens with real estate and bank accounts held in this manner. Similarly, anything with a beneficiary designation passes outside probate - this could be a "transfer on death" (TOD) on an investment account, a "pay on death" (POD) on a bank account, or a beneficiary named on an insurance policy, IRA, or annuity account. Sometimes bank accounts will have a beneficiary designation "in trust for" or ITF. These all pass to the named individual(s) upon the death.

I've had people who have put a great deal of thought and effort to draft a will with the intent their property all be divided equally among their children. But they may place one child as a joint owner on their bank account for convenience. That bank account then will belong, in its entirety, to that one child. That child may or may not share the money with siblings. If they do share it, that money shared will then be a gift among siblings and could possibly have unintended tax consequences.

I have also seen people add a child as POD or TOD because it was recommended. Sometimes these people expect the instruction in their will to control. The will does not control if there are joint ownerships and beneficiary designations.

It would be possible to make all beneficiary designations mirror images of what is in the will. The problem of joint ownership, however, cannot be overcome and cannot be changed after death. The child who is joint owner has no obligation to share the money. He or she may not feel as kindly to your other children as you did. Another risk here is even if that child intended to share according to your wishes, the money is rightfully theirs until they give it away. If they have creditors trying to collect, or if they are in a bankruptcy, it is likely the money will go to that joint owner's creditors.

As part of estate planning, your attorney can review assets, titles, and beneficiary designations and advise you on how not to inadvertently disinherit an heir.

2. Intentional Disinheritance of a Special Needs Child

Many times, the parent of a special needs child will hear advice that they should disinherit the special needs child. The reason is that if the child is receiving government benefits (things like SSI, AHCCCS, ALTCS, Medi-Cal, and other needs-based benefits), they will risk losing those benefits if they receive the inheritance. Those needs-based benefits usually require the recipient have minimal assets and/or income.

It is true your special needs child could lose benefits if they receive the inheritance outright. But rather than disinheriting them, it might be better to consider a trust for them. The law allows a special needs trust or supplemental needs trust, written a specific way to allow benefits that would not result in losing other government benefits. Such a trust can greatly enhance that child's life.

3. Misuse of a Power of Attorney

Powers of Attorneys are dangerous (but often necessary) instruments. It is important to realize the Power ends at death. Sometimes the person who is named as power of attorney will continue to use that document to make withdrawals, pay bills, and other actions, after the date of death. This is not permitted and can get you in trouble. Under Arizona law, and most other states, if someone misuses a power of attorney, there can be very severe penalties, including double damages, and even being disinherited by law.

Another way I see POAs misused is when the person named as POA makes a gift to himself. It is not permissible to use a POA to gift to yourself. The principal (the person for whom you are POA) may be perfectly fine with it. But that doesn't matter. For example, I had a client who was POA for her father. She and her father went to MVD because her father wanted to transfer title of his vehicle to her. The father was tired and told her to go ahead and sign for him and she did, as POA. That was later questioned, after the father's death, and cost a great deal of money in legal fees. If the principal has capacity, he should be signing for the transfer himself. Any transaction that appears to benefit the agent, is highly suspicious if the agent carried it out.

It is always less expensive to plan properly and get good advice from an experienced and knowledgeable estate planning attorney. Yes, attorneys can be expensive. But many will answer questions, review documents, and advise on these matters for a reasonable fee. It is cheaper to buy an hour of an attorney's time now, than many hours to straighten the mess out later.

25

HOSPICE

Hospice, as practiced in the United States, is based on a philosophy designed to support physical, psychosocial and spiritual needs of terminally ill patients and their families and significant others.

According to Medicare, "Hospice is a special way of caring for people who are terminally ill, and for their family. This care includes physical care and counseling. Hospice care is given by a public agency or private company approved by Medicare. It is for all age groups, including children, adults, and the elderly during their final stages of life. The goal of hospice is to care for you and your family, not to cure your illness."

Among services provided by Medicare, hospice includes medical and support services such as nursing care, social services, doctor services, counseling, homemaker services, and various other types of services. A team approach is utilized and includes doctors, nurses, home health aides, social workers, counselors, chaplains, and trained volunteers, with most care provided in the patient's home. Patients may also have hospice care in a hospice facility, hospital, nursing home, assisted living facility or adult care home.

In 1978, Senator Edward Kennedy said: "Hospice is many things. Hospice is home care with inpatient back-up facilities. Hospice is pain control. Hospice is skilled nursing. Hospice is a doctor and a clergyman coming to your home . . . But most of all, hospice is the humanization of our health care system."

Although the concept has been around for thousands of years, the modern hospice movement has often been attributed to a British nurse turned physician (and who also held a degree in social work), Dame Cicely Saunders, who established the St. Christopher's Hospice in London in 1967. Dame Cicely assembled a team consisting of physicians, nurses, chaplains, counselors and physical therapists to deliver care to the dying. The program at St. Christopher's consists of both residential and home care components.

Hospice began in the United States in New Haven Connecticut. The Hospice of New Haven was founded by Florence Wald, former Dean of Yale University's School of Nursing. Ms. Wald had heard Dr. Saunders lecture in the 1960's, left Yale, and worked for several years at St. Christopher's before returning to the United States and starting the hospice movement here. The Connecticut Hospice was incorporated in 1971, began seeing home patients in 1974 and opened an inpatient facility in 1979.

In 1982, the Hospice Medicare benefit was enacted as part of the Tax Equity and Fiscal Responsibility Act, and Medicare has provided funding that has fueled the hospice movement ever since. The Medicare entitlement became permanent in 1986. In 1986, the Consolidated Omnibus Budget Reconciliation Act allowed Medicaid to pay for hospice care. At that time, there were 1,505 hospices in the United States.

Over the years, Medicare guidelines have been established and criteria developed as part of the constant evolution shaping the growth and development of hospice care. These guidelines have also provided the framework for most private insurance companies who offer hospice as a benefit. The underlying principal of hospice care is no curative treatment be provided for the diagnosis that led to hospice qualification. Therefore, patients do not typically receive chemotherapy, rehabilitative or restorative treatment or surgical intervention. Such treatment may be available, however, if the goal of the treatment is to alleviate symptoms and promote comfort, but not cure the disease. For example, if the patient is admitted for cancer and pain is caused by pressure from a growing tumor, chemotherapy or radiation may be used to shrink the tumor if the goal is to alleviate the pain and not to cure the cancer.

Hospice focuses on palliative care, or treatment of symptoms; anything that will provide comfort. The most common symptoms treated are pain, difficulty breathing, nausea and vomiting and fatigue. Palliative care is also offered in settings outside of hospice and sometimes in conjunction with curative treatments.

In order to qualify for hospice care, certain criteria must be met. Among those criteria is a physician certification the patient's life expectancy is six months or less without treatment. Of course, the physician does not know how long a person will live. The decision will be based on a number of objective criteria suggest a limited life expectancy of six months or less. It is possible the patient will improve or will continue to decline yet not die within the six months. If improving, the patient can be discharged from hospice. There is no penalty for going on and off hospice many times over a period of years; it is also possible the patient will continue on hospice for longer than six months.

Since hospice treatment is related to a specific "hospice diagnosis," a patient can be on hospice for one diagnosis, while the patient continues to receive life-prolonging treatment for another disease. For example, a patient may meet hospice criteria for a diagnosis of end stage dementia. So the patient is admitted, hospice bills for their service, and the patient does not receive aggressive dementia treatment. However, the patient may also have a cardiac diagnosis for which aggressive, life-prolonging treatment is provided by another provider. Or, the patient may also have end stage renal disease and be on dialysis all while remaining on hospice for dementia. It seems contradictory, but occasionally happens while fitting within guidelines. These guidelines may be changing in the not-too-distant future.

Two physicians, the patient's attending and the hospice medical director, must initially certify the patient meets hospice criteria. The initial certification period is for 90 days. The patient must then be certified for a second period of 90 days and after that, an unlimited number of 60 day certification periods. As long as the patient is deemed to meet criteria at the times of recertification, that patient can remain on hospice far longer than six months.

All of hospice care is billed at a daily rate, subject to a yearly cap, based on four levels of care. These rates are adjusted for geographic area. The rates are all inclusive and the daily rate for each level is paid regardless of the amount of services, supplies, equipment or medication required.

Routine Home Care is the most common level – 96% of hospice patients are at this level. This level of care can be utilized whether a patient is in a facility or in her own house – wherever they live is considered home. Routine home care generally includes intermittent visits from a social worker, home health aide, chaplain and/or counselor. Volunteers are often involved. Medications, equipment and therapies may also be provided. The nurse may visit once or twice a week and the home health aide may visit two or three times a week. There is not any provision for blocks of time to be spent with the patient, although home health services for help with personal care may be provided over an hour or two. The 2016 basic daily payment rate for Routine Level is either $186.84 or $146.83. The higher amount is for the first 60 days. Other factors affecting the rate may include whether required quality data has been submitted, and it is further adjusted for the geographic area, based on local wages.

Continuous Nursing Care at Home is provided when the patients' symptoms become uncontrollable and a skilled person must be present to manage symptoms. To bill at the Continuous Care rate, a certified nurse assistant or nurse must be present for at least eight out of 24 hours. Often, it is necessary to have someone present for much more than eight hours if symptoms are out of control. The amount paid by Medicare for Continuous Home Care in 2016 is approximately $944.79, adjusted geographically.

Inpatient Care in a hospice facility can also be utilized for uncontrolled symptoms. Some hospices have their own facility. Many hospices will contract beds at a nursing home, hospital, or even another hospice's facility. The 2016 daily rate for General Inpatient Care is $720.11, with adjustments adding or subtracting.

Continuous Nursing Care and General Inpatient Care are used in crises when symptoms cannot be managed otherwise. Although the payment levels are high, these are often less cost-effective for hospices than Routine Home Care. Both Continuous Nursing Care and General Inpatient Care are labor intensive and otherwise costly for the hospice. Some criticism has been leveled at the hospice industry because, although hospices must offer and have available these levels for crisis care, some hospices do not use them. In fact, 18% of hospices did not provide either level to any patient in a 2012 study.

Respite Care occurs when the patient has been receiving care at home, and the caregivers at home need a short break. This is a temporary placement in a facility and can last up to five days before the patient returns home. Inpatient Respite Care is paid at a rate of $170.08 or $173.48. All rates quoted will have geographic adjustments and possibly some other adjustments, but the numbers will be very close to those cited.

There are also some caps on payment imposed by Medicare. For example, hospices are precluded from receiving payment for inpatient care that exceeds 20% of the total patient care days for that hospice. A second cap imposed is known as the aggregate cap. This cap is arrived at by multiplying the cap amount by the number of beneficiaries (patients) who elected hospice care in that period. In 2014, that cap amount was $26,725.79.

It is obvious that hospice can be a very profitable business. In fact, currently, hospices treat over a million patients a year and take in $17 billion dollars a year. Most of that money comes from Medicare. As with most government programs, hospice began with the best intentions and has provided tremendous benefit to a great many individuals and families. But as with anything, some people have found ways to abuse the system. Those abuses lead to greater regulation which will invariably hurt innocent people, mainly patients. The majority of hospice providers and hospice workers are doing excellent work.

There are several things to look for when choosing a hospice. One consideration is to ask about the availability of an inpatient unit. Does the hospice have their own facility? Do they contract with another facility or facilities? Which ones? How often do they use either General Inpatient Care or Continuous Nursing Care? You can also speak to people who operate support groups or to your local Area Agency on Aging to get recommendations from them regarding hospice. Most often, a referral is made by a doctor's office or hospital discharge planner or social worker. It is a good idea to speak with more than one hospice before deciding. As with anything else, however, it will depend on the commitment and compassion of the individual caregivers.

Remember, too, patients can change hospices once in each benefit period. The hospices will work out any billing issues. While on hospice, if you have concerns with the care or services, you are free to contact another hospice and tell them you are interested in transferring care. You will then have an opportunity to meet with a representative of that hospice and decide if that option seems better. With hospice, the patient and the family should be involved in making decisions and guiding the care. In fact, the patient and family members should be considered part of the hospice's interdisciplinary team.

Hospice is a wonderful benefit. Like anything else, it is not appropriate for everyone and is not always the best choice. There are many varieties of hospice and while one hospice may be perfect for one patient, another hospice may be more appropriate for someone else. It is important to be a wise consumer. It is also important to educate yourself in advance – thinking about hospice is part of planning and it is best done well before the need arises.

26

WHAT'S NEXT?

I'd like to talk about the future. I want to briefly discuss what's next for the area of estate planning law, and what's next for you.

What's next for estate planning law:

Many people, especially attorneys, have a misconception estate planning is not an exciting area of law. Law students often look for areas that appear more "exciting" such as criminal defense, or prosecution, personal injury, mass torts, and class actions. These are areas that are often featured in television shows, movies, and sometimes highly publicized real cases. People sometimes believe estate planning involves no more than drafting documents or filling in templates. Nothing is farther from the truth.

Estate planning is one of the few areas of law that is rapidly changing. Efforts to keep up with technological and social changes are shaping estate planning law. Advances include cutting edge topics such as digital assets, medical advances prolonging life and even modifying the definition of death, assisted suicide, euthanasia, reproductive advances that can result in conception after someone dies, non-traditional relationships such as same sex marriage, blended families, single and three parent families, and so much more. The makeup of a family is ever changing and has become very complex. This raises issues for planning.

Single parent families, though not new, raise often overlooked planning problems such as naming a guardian. Sometimes, there is another living parent who may or may not be an appropriate person to take custody if the custodial parent dies or becomes incapacitated. Or maybe, it is a single person who adopted children and there is truly just one legal parent. Planning is different in every one of these situations.

We also have a much larger number of blended families. We used to refer to these as "his, hers, and ours" referring to having children from each spouse's previous marriage and also some from the current one. Sometimes, there are children from more than two different partners. Blended families present unique challenges for estate planning in order to meet the needs of a surviving spouse, while preserving the inheritance of the deceased spouse's children. This is a delicate balance which often takes sophisticated planning to assure smooth transitions and minimized conflict.

In 2015, an Iowa court case came about after a daughter had been appointed guardian over her mother who had dementia. The case involved issues regarding the step-father having sex with his wife, the guardian's mother. The guardian pursued charges of sexual abuse against the step-father and a legal question focused on whether an incapacitated person has the ability to consent to sexual contact with their spouse. The lights of the courtroom shone on this case for several weeks. These are estate planning issues that were not contemplated 20 years ago. In this case, the issues were complicated by the existence of a blended family. Proper planning can prevent many issues like this.

What about cases of frozen sperm or embryos? It is now possible to conceive a child after the person providing sperm or eggs has died. Is that child an heir? Does that child need to be provided for from the deceased donor's estate? What about social security survivor benefits? What if the donor of sperm or eggs is alive? What about people who have frozen embryos and get divorced?

There are cases of people who have made agreements to donate sperm for another couple. However, that donor must closely follow the law to avoid having to be responsible at some point for child support, or the child may be entitled to a portion of the donor's estate when the donor dies. All these things need to be addressed as part of estate planning.

The problems faced with some single-parent families are clear, but what about a child with three parents? Yes, they exist through a procedure called mitochondrial replacement. Genetic material from a third person is used to try to eliminate a genetic disease in a child conceived by two other people. Does the lucky child have rights to inheritance from all three parents? Do all three have responsibilities? The law is undecided.

What happens when people "lend" genetic material for someone else to use? What rights of inheritance do posthumously conceived children have? Sperm can be extracted from someone recently deceased and used to inseminate a wife or girlfriend. There have been cases when a man is diagnosed with a terminal illness and sperm is taken while he is alive and frozen to be used by his wife after he dies. Or sperm can be frozen for years after a donor's death before it is used. Does the length of time between conception and death matter in terms of inheritance, social security benefits, and other insurance? These are estate planning issues.

Other issues that impact estate planning include life sustaining technology and assisted suicide. Your estate planning documents can clearly express your wishes in terms of life prolongation (or shortening) and directly address issues about hospice, palliative care, organ donation, autopsy, and disposition of remains. Do you want your ashes blasted into outer-space? Or would you like your head cryogenically frozen?

Estate planning and governing law are very much racing to keep up with technological and social development. Exciting things are happening and things have never changed at such a rapid pace.

What's next for you:

By purchasing and reading this book, you have demonstrated an interest in these important topics and for that, I thank you. But, further action is required.

If you have an estate plan, take time to review it and make sure it is current and expresses your wishes and your situation as they are today. If the plan is more than two years old, have it reviewed by an experienced estate planning attorney. If your plan is a do-it-yourself plan or an internet plan, have it reviewed by an experienced estate planning attorney. Remember all attorneys are not the same. Find an attorney with experience and training in this area. And when I say training, I mean an attorney who is actively keeping his knowledge and skills updated to reflect the ever changing status of the law and society. This is a field that requires constant updating of knowledge and skills. See the chapter Choosing Your Team.

Estate plan review does not have to be crazy expensive. Some estate planning attorneys will meet with you, free of charge, to review and evaluate a plan. Many will charge a reasonable consultation fee for that service. It is well worth the fee to meet with an attorney. This could save much more in the future. It could mean the difference between your wishes being carried out and not. A good plan can fit almost any budget. Finding an attorney who offers estate planning maintenance plans can be a great way to minimize updating costs and assuring the plan is maintained. Some attorneys offer a maintenance plan with an annual fee that includes routine updating.

Planning is crucial, but not all plans work. If you created your plan many years ago (and have not updated it), if you got it off the internet or copied someone else's documents and changed the names, the sense of security you feel is false. Get it fixed. Consult an experienced estate planning attorney. If you have used a reputable attorney, if something does go wrong, it can probably be fixed. If you have done it yourself, there is no recourse and you, or your survivors, will have to live with it and pay for it.

Make sure your parents, your adult children, and anyone close to you has a plan and has it reviewed and maintained. Share the information from this book with anyone you care about.

Lastly, talk about these things. Don't keep your plan a secret. You don't have to tell everyone about it, including all of the beneficiaries, but make sure those closest to you know where to find your paperwork. Let key people know their roles as successor trustee or personal representative.

Make sure your agents under your health care power of attorney know what you want. Have the conversation with those closest to you.

It is my firm belief that life is far richer when we have thoughtfully planned for our futures and the futures of those we care most about.

READING AND RESOURCES

These are books from my personal library, and a few websites, that deal with areas of disability, dementia and death. I recommend all of these for various reasons. Some are instructive, enlightening, and useful. Others are enormously interesting and appeal to my insatiable curiosity about the subject.

<u>On Death and Dying</u> by Elisabeth Kubler-Ross, M.D. (1969) www.ekrfoundation.org/

This is the classic book about death and the dying process. I believe this was the first time anyone laid out stages through which a dying person passes. These stages have also been applied to families and to the grieving process.

<u>Saying Goodbye: How Families Can Find Renewal Through Loss</u> by Barbara Okun, Ph.D. and Joseph Nowinski, Ph.D. (2011) www.josephnowinski.com

Here, two psychologists review how dying has changed since 1969 (when <u>On Death and Dying</u> was written) and describe five stages of family grief, explaining and responding to modern death and dying. Much practical information is offered on dealing with each stage.

<u>All My Children Wear Fur Coats</u> by Peggy Hoyt, J.D., M.B.A. (2008) www.hoytbryan.com

A comprehensive description of planning for your pets in the event of the owner's disability or death, and much more regarding pets as survivors and even pet loss.

<u>The 36-Hour Day</u> by Nancy L. Mace, M.A., and Peter V. Rabins, M.D., M.P.H. (1981)

Now a classic. An incredible book for families to help deal with dementia in a family member, through all stages

The American Way of Death by Jessica Mitford (1963)

This is another great classic that turned the funeral industry upside down. A shocking expose that led to major changes in the funeral industry.

Final Rights: Reclaiming the American Way of Death by Joshua Slocum and Lisa Carlson (2011)   finalrights.org

The funeral consumer movement, started by Jessica Mitford, is experiencing a resurgence, thanks to Joshua Slocum and Lisa Carlson. Slocum is the Executive Director of the Funeral Consumers Alliance. This book looks at laws and regulations impacting what happens with us after we die. A state-by-state approach creates a valuable legal guide.

A Good Goodbye: Funeral Planning for Those Who Don't Plan to Die by Gail Rubin (2010) agoodgoodbye.com

Gail Rubin calls herself "The Doyenne of Death ™" In this light and entertaining book, she covers many aspects of planning, communicating those plans, and creative ways of remembering. There is even a section dealing with pets.

Death for Beginners: Your No-Nonsense, Money-Saving Guide to Planning for the Inevitable by Karen Jones (2010) deathforbeginners.com

Another very entertaining treatment of planning for death, with a strong focus on the creative and unusual. The book also has several pages of checklists to help plan.

Being Mortal: Medicine and What Matters in the End by Atul Gawande, M.D. (2014) AtulGawande.com

A beautifully written comprehensive study of growing old and dying, from a surgeon's perspective. A wonderful mix of research and anecdote brings dying to life.

Dying Well: Peace and Possibilities At the End of Life by Ira Byock, M.D. (1997) irabyock.org

Another incredible perspective on the process of dying. Dr. Byock, a hospice physician, teaches us from the lessons he has learned from patients.

Final Gifts: Understanding the Special Awareness, Needs, and Communications of the Dying by Maggie Callahan and Patricia Kelley (1997) MaggieCallanan.com

Touching stories of hospice patients from the perspective of nurses who care for them. Now a classic.

Life After Life by Raymond A. Moody, Jr., M.D. (1975)

The classic about near death experiences presented as a study conducted by a leading psychiatrist.

Evidence of Eternity: Communicating with Spirits for Proof of the Afterlife by Mark Anthony (2015) Healgriefwithbelief.com

Mark is an attorney and a psychic medium who presents the case for life after death.

The Boomer Burden: Dealing With Your Parents' Lifetime Accumulation of Stuff by Julie Hall (2007) TheEstatelady.com

A practical guide to downsizing, cleaning out, getting rid of, and dividing the tangible personal property of aging and deceased parents. This book can help keep the family together by dealing creatively with one of the greatest sources of conflict – personal property.

Stiff: The Curious Lives of Human Cadavers by Mary Roach (2003)
Maryroach.net

This is an amazingly entertaining book about all the ways you can make yourself useful after you die.

Dead and Buried: The Horrible History of Bodysnatching by Norman Adams (1972)

Don't ask me what attracts me to this stuff. But I love this book about what medical students used to have to do to learn their craft.

What Happens When You Die: From Your Last Breath to the First Spadeful by Robert T. Hatch (1981)

A step-by-step description of the process we go through once dead. Mr. Hatch discusses embalming, mummification, religious aspects, and what goes on at a funeral home. Learn to differentiate among algor mortis, rigor mortis, and livor mortis. And much more in this thin, fascinating book.

Freezing People is (Not) Easy: My Adventures in Cryonics by Bob Nelson (2014)

The story of freezing the first people (and inadvertently thawing some of them).

A Short & Happy Guide to Elder Law by Kenney F. Hegland & Robert B. Fleming (2013)

A light and whimsical approach to legal (and some not so legal) aspects of aging. A wide variety of issues are presented in a fun and easily understood manner.

WEBSITES

AARP.org

Up to date information featuring End Of Life Planning resources

CaringInfo.org

Access Advance Directive documents from almost all states.

DonateLife.net

Non-Profit Organization dedicated to providing donation and transplantation education and facilitation.

Funerals.org

The website of the Funeral Consumers Alliance ™ with a wealth of information about the funeral industry and links to local chapters.

TheConversationProject.org

Non-Profit Organization focused on helping people talk about their wishes for end-of-life care.

TucsonEstatePlanning.com

Ronald Zack's website providing education and resources regarding estate planning and elder law.

ABOUT THE AUTHOR

Ronald Zack is a partner at the Udall Law Firm in Tucson, Arizona and focuses his practice on the areas of estate planning, elder law, and probate. In addition to his Juris Doctorate degree, Ron earned a Master of Arts degree in Linguistics and a Master of Science degree in Nursing Education. He maintains his nursing license, has had extensive experience in Hospice and Palliative nursing, and continues to remain involved in hospice nursing. Currently, he is vice president of the Arizona Gerontological Nursing Association, president of the Pima County Bar Association, and serves on the board of Pima Council on Aging, the local Area Agency on Aging. He is a member of WealthCounsel®, the National Academy of Elder Law Attorneys, the Hospice and Palliative Nurses Association, and is admitted to practice law in both Arizona and California.

Ron is a founder of a non-profit corporation – Hospice Education and Legal Partnership, Inc. which provides pro bono and reduced fee legal services to people with terminal illness and their families and caregivers. Donations are appreciated at hospicelegalline.org.

Outside the law office, Ron is an amateur magician and published poet. He is also the weekly host and executive producer of Law Review Radio, a trusted source for legal news, entertaining legal stories, and interviews with intriguing people who are affected by the law.

Made in the USA
Middletown, DE
27 September 2016